Applied jQuery

DEVELOP AND DESIGN

Jay Blanchard

Peachpit
Press

Applied jQuery: Develop and Design
Jay Blanchard

Peachpit Press
1249 Eighth Street
Berkeley, CA 94710
510/524-2178
510/524-2221 (fax)

Find us on the Web at: www.peachpit.com
To report errors, please send a note to: errata@peachpit.com
Peachpit Press is a division of Pearson Education.
Copyright © 2012 by Jay Blanchard

Editor: Rebecca Gulick
Development and Copy Editor: Anne Marie Walker
Technical Reviewer: Jesse R. Castro
Production Coordinator: Myrna Vladic
Compositor: Danielle Foster
Proofreader: Patricia Pane
Indexer: Valerie Haynes-Perry
Cover design: Aren Straiger
Interior design: Mimi Heft

ISBN 13: 978-0-321-77256-5
ISBN 10:   0-321-77256-3

9 8 7 6 5 4 3 2 1

Printed and bound in the United States of America

To Mom, who taught me there was magic in books,

and to Dad, who taught me there was magic in me.

ACKNOWLEDGMENTS

Projects like this are not possible without the support and understanding of a lot of people, something I really didn't understand when first embarking on the journey to create a book. Saying "thank you" isn't nearly enough, but I hope that you all understand how much I appreciate you!

Even with the blender of life roaring around us, Connie Kay, Kaitlyn, Brittany, Zach, Karla, and Morgan provided more love and support than you can imagine. I love you all!

To Rebecca Gulick, thank you for believing in me and helping a dream to come true!

To Anne Marie Walker, enough cannot be said about your gentle firmness, guidance, and subtle humor. I am eternally grateful to you!

To Jesse Castro, thanks for keeping me on the straight and narrow. Your insight, technical abilities, and encouragement blow me away!

To Larry Ullman, thanks for being the Ford Prefect to my Arthur Dent and guiding me through the galaxy! I kept my towel on my desk the whole time!

To Francis Govers, the twists and turns in my life are made all the more bearable by knowing that you are just a phone call or an e-mail away. Best friends don't get any better!

To the folks who have made up the teams of developers that I have worked with day in and day out, thank you for making me a better programmer and a better person! Your willingness to look over my shoulder and teach me something new is treasured beyond measure.

To the jQuery community, you are an amazing group of people, and I am honored to share electrons with you!

CONTENTS

INTRODUCTION

As Web designers, you are painstakingly compelled to grab Web surfers' attention as quickly as possible and then keep them on your site to absorb the content. In addition to the product, service, or information that you are providing, the site must be visually attractive and offer stimulating (and valuable) interaction. The jQuery library is the main ingredient for providing the icing on your Web-site cake. If applied well, the effects of jQuery will convince visitors and application users to click around and sample all of your content.

The trick is learning how to combine jQuery with other markup and languages effectively. You must gain knowledge in a wide range of disciplines, like HTML (HyperText Markup Language) and CSS (Cascading Style Sheets), to know how to properly mix in the right amount of jQuery. The goal of this book is to give you the knowledge to bring the HTML, CSS, and jQuery ingredients together to create compelling interactivity to your Web sites and applications.

Throughout the book, I'll also show you ways to use PHP, a popular server-side scripting language, and MySQL, a relational database product, to enhance your overall development and supercharge your applications. Both technologies translate easily to other Web development languages.

WHAT IS JQUERY?

Announced in 2006 by its creator, John Resig, jQuery quickly gained popularity and support as a new way to use JavaScript to interact with HTML and CSS. jQuery's simple selectors mimicked CSS selectors, making the library familiar and easy to learn for designers and developers alike. The jQuery library erased the worry that Web developers had suffered through when trying to create interactive sites across a wide range of browsers by handling most browser compatibility issues behind the scenes.

Topping off those two features is the shortened syntax used by jQuery. The following example shows how you would select an element based on its id attribute using jQuery:

```
$('#foo');
```

The jQuery selector is much shorter as opposed to the same example in old-school JavaScript:

```
document.getElementByID('foo');
```

It's no wonder that the Web-development community embraced jQuery's "write less, do more" mantra. Couple the simplicity of jQuery with its ability to support complex animations and achieve stupendous effects, and you get a JavaScript library that is flexible and capable of empowering you to provide your Web site visitors with an outstanding interactive experience.

WHO THIS BOOK IS FOR

This book is aimed at beginning to intermediate Web developers, but it doesn't matter where you are in your journey as a designer or developer. You should find examples in this book that will help you to bring your Web pages and applications to life with jQuery. It helps if you have a basic knowledge of HTML, CSS, JavaScript, and jQuery, but it is not necessary because the examples are fully baked and ready to go.

WHAT I USED

As of this writing, jQuery 1.5 had been released and is used for all of the examples in the book. You can download it at www.jquery.com. It is also available on the book's Web site at www.appliedjquery.com.

HTML, CSS, and JavaScript files are all plain-text files that you can create and edit in any plain-text editor.

Examples were all tested in Firefox 3 and Internet Explorer 8, with an occasional peek in Safari and Google Chrome.

WHERE TO FIND THE CODE

All of the code examples for the book are available from the *Applied jQuery* Web site at www.appliedjquery.com/downloads. There you can download a Zip file containing all of the examples, graphics, and other collateral needed to follow along.

The examples are arranged by chapter within the Zip file and include all of the necessary jQuery files to make the examples work right out of the box.

However, even though all of the files are available for download, I encourage you to type out each example as you progress through the book. Taking a hands-on approach will help you to learn how all of the technologies fit together and will reinforce the concepts in your brain.

LET'S GET STARTED

It's time for you to jump right in and get started learning how to use jQuery. In the first chapter I'll give you some good rules and tools to get you headed in the right direction for sweetening your Web development efforts with jQuery.

i

WELCOME TO jQUERY

WELCOME TO jQUERY

jQuery is one of the most popular JavaScript libraries in use today because it lets you build JavaScript Web pages and Web applications quickly and easily, accomplishing in a single line of code something that would have required dozens of lines of JavaScript code. Grab yourself a computer and the handful of tools outlined below, and then dig into the following six chapters.

jQUERY

jQuery, which is free to download and use, comes in the form of a single .js file that you link to from your Web page, and your code accesses the library by calling various jQuery functions. Go to jquery. com and download the jQuery library.

jQUERY UI

Next, you'll want to download the jQuery UI library from jQueryUI.com. This will equip you with some core interaction plugins as well as many UI widgets that I'll discuss later in the book.

TEXT EDITOR

You'll be doing some scripting, so get yourself a good text editor. Windows users typically opt for Microsoft Notepad or Notepad++, while Mac users often rely on BBEdit from Bare Bones Software.

BROWSER

Chances are you've already got a standards-compliant browser installed. Popular options are the latest versions of Microsoft Internet Explorer, Mozilla Firefox, Apple Safari, Google Chrome, and Opera.

TROUBLESHOOTER

I rely heavily on the Firebug Web development tool for troubleshooting. Go to http://getfirebug.com and get a version that's specific to your browser. It's 100% free and open source, and you'll be grateful you've got it installed when something goes wrong.

TESTING ENVIRONMENT

Rather than using an actual hosted Web site to test your jQuery creations, use a testing environment that's local on your own computer. I use XAMPP, which you can download from http://apachefriends.org.

1

INTRODUCING
jQUERY

Rich, interactive Web sites that use semantic markup and unobtrusive technologies like Cascading Style Sheets (CSS) and JavaScript are becoming the de facto standard in Web development. Designers and developers are looking for new and better ways to bring their creations to life, and libraries like jQuery make this goal easily attainable.

To get started properly with jQuery, you need to equip yourself with the appropriate tools and concepts. So, I've gathered those tools for you and will help you to learn how to use them.

This chapter will give you a firm grasp of the basics of jQuery and the tools that will make working with jQuery straightforward. Also included are some tips for getting the most out of jQuery. But first things first; let's start with a "Hello World" example jQuery style.

MAKING **jQUERY WORK**

The strength of the jQuery library is its ability to interact with elements in your Web pages that you are already familiar with. Markup tags, class declarations, and attribute information in your Web pages can be easily connected to jQuery by using the simple concept of selectors.

A jQuery selector will wrap an element or set of elements into an object. Once you have created the jQuery object, you can effectively apply a multitude of jQuery methods to that object to create animations, send information to and from the server, or perform object manipulation.

No book on programming is worth its salt if it doesn't have a "Hello World!" example. To illustrate the power and flexibility of jQuery's selectors, let's create a "Hello World!" example.

NOTE: The Hello World code is the only code example not available in the download from the book's Web site. The reason is that I think it is very important that you type this one in yourself. Comments are also included in the example.

1. Start by establishing the basic markup for the HTML page:

```
<!DOCTYPE>
<html lang="en">
    <head>
        <meta charset="utf-8" />
        <title>Hello World - jQuery Style</title>
```

2. Be sure to include the jQuery source file. Without this file none of the jQuery code will operate:

```
<script type="text/javascript"
➝ src="jquery-1.5.min.js"></script>
```

3. Open a script tag to give the jQuery code a place to live within the page:

```
<script type="text/javascript">
```

4. The jQuery functions that you are creating need to be available to run after the Web page has finished loading all of its elements. To accomplish this, you wrap the jQuery code in a *document ready* function. Just as it implies, the code wrapped in the function becomes available to run when the Web document is ready:

```
$(document).ready(function() {
```

5. Create the first selector. This selector will get the markup element in the page having an id attribute equal to first. All id attributes are selected in jQuery (and CSS) by prepending the hash (#) sign to the information contained within the id attribute. You'll follow the selector with jQuery's html method by chaining the html method to the selector. This method will place the markup <h1>Hello World!</h1> into the selected element:

```
/* write 'Hello World! to the first div */

$('#first').html('<h1>Hello World!</h1>');
```

Chaining is the term used to describe applying one or more methods to jQuery objects. Chaining gives you a wide variety of possibilities to combine methods to create unique interactions for your Web-site visitors.

6. For this example, you'll create one additional method that connects, or *binds,* an event handler to a selector to create an action. The event handler will accept an action and perform additional jQuery functions to other selected elements. Start this portion of the example by binding jQuery's click handler to an element with an id of link:

```
/* a clickable 'Hello World!' example */

$('#link').click(function() {
```

The click method exposes a handler function that allows you to build a string of actions that will be triggered by the click method.

7. Set up a selector for the element with an id of greeting and apply the html method to it:

```
$('#greeting').html('<h1>Hello Again!</h1>');
```

8. Close out the jQuery code with the proper braces, brackets, and script tags:

```
        });
    });
    </script>
```

Pay close attention to braces and brackets when you create jQuery code. It is critically important that each opening bracket or brace have a matching closing bracket or brace.

9. Finish up the head section of the markup and open the body of the Web page:

```
    </head>
    <body>
```

10. Create an HTML div with an id of first. The initial jQuery selector that you created previously will interact with this element, adding the HTML markup that was specified between the div tags:

```
    <div id="first"></div>
```

11. Create another HTML div with an id of second. You did not write any selectors for this element; it is just being used as a container for other elements:

```
    <div id="second">
```

12. Create an anchor tag and give it an id of link. You wrote jQuery code earlier that will handle the link when it is clicked by a user:

```
    <a href="#" id="link">Click Me!</a><br />
```

13. Create a span element with an id of greeting. When the link is clicked, the selector for greeting will apply the HTML markup you specified between the span tags:

```
    <span id="greeting"></span>
```

14. Complete the page by closing out the markup tags properly:

```
        </div>
    </body>
</html>
```

FIGURE 1.1 The "Hello World!" message appears when the page loads, and the "Hello Again!" message appears when the link is clicked.

15. Save the file as *hello_world.html* and load it into your Web browser. If you have been diligent with your typing, you will be rewarded with a Web page identical to the one shown in **Figure 1.1**.

This example is just a small taste of how you can connect jQuery to elements in your Web pages to provide information and interactivity. The example also demonstrates how you can add elements to your Web pages using jQuery.

To work with jQuery effectively, you need to know how to work with all of the elements in a Web page and how they are assembled into a document.

A document?

That is absolutely correct: Web pages are documents that are intended for display in Web browsers. Because Web pages are documents, they follow some of the same rules that paper documents follow, and those rules are provided by the master document—the Document Object Model (DOM).

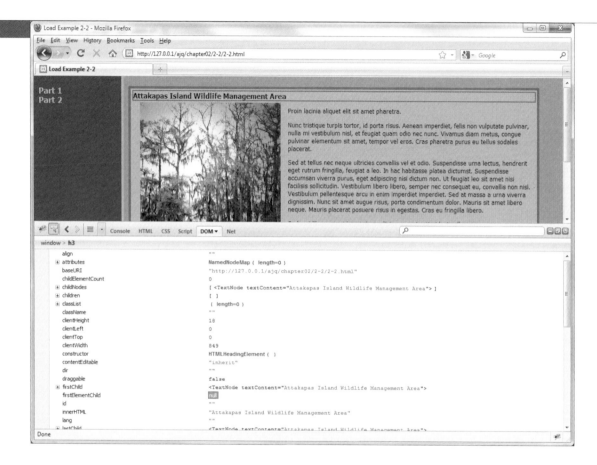

FIGURE 1.2 Examining the DOM using Firebug with Firefox.

At the heart of all of your Web pages is an API (Application Programming Interface) that describes everything on the page. It is the DOM. The DOM provides information for each element on the page, including styles associated with elements. The information in the DOM is stored in a tree-like structure.

Several DOM inspector applications are available either as stand-alone applications or as add-ins to many popular Web browsers. **Figure 1.2** shows the DOM inspector available with Firebug.

```
<div id="information">
    <ul> // child of <div id="information">
        <li> // child of <ul>, sibling to the other <li>
            <a href="foo.html"> // child of nearest <li>
                <img src="bar.jpg" /> // child of <a href="foo.html">
            </a>
        </li>
        <li> // child of <ul>, sibling to the other <li>
            <a href="glorp.html"> // child of nearest <li>
                <img src="murkle.jpg" /> // child of <a href="glorp.html">

            </a>
        </li>
    </ul>
</div>
```

FIGURE 1.3 An outline of the relationships between the elements in the list.

The DOM API is what allows languages like JavaScript and libraries like jQuery to interact with elements in your Web pages. You can use libraries like jQuery to virtually climb up and down the DOM tree to locate, add, remove, and modify elements. Because you'll be using jQuery to interact with the DOM, including adding and removing elements from it, you need to become familiar with how the DOM is constructed. You don't need to become an expert on the DOM, but you should know enough about the DOM to recognize what is going on when you manipulate it with jQuery.

Knowing the DOM becomes critically important when you start working with jQuery's parent and child type selectors. You must understand the relationship between the elements in the DOM so that you can effectively manipulate those elements. Consider the following HTML markup:

```
<div id="information">
    <ul>
        <li><a href="foo.html"><img src="bar.jpg" /></a></li>
        <li><a href="glorp.html"><img src="murkle.jpg" /></a></li>
    </ul>
</div>
```

To know how to travel up and down the DOM tree, you must know what the relationships are between the elements. **Figure 1.3** shows how those relationships are defined.

LINE BREAKS AND COMMENTS

Because JavaScript allows you to continue code through line breaks, jQuery will, too. This means that you can spread chained jQuery methods over several lines. Spreading lengthy chains over multiple lines makes the jQuery methods visually easier to follow and troubleshoot. Quite often you'll see jQuery chains similar to the following example:

```
var nextImage = $('img[src="bar.jpg"]') // define the
→ starting point
    .closest('li') // travel up to the closest list item
    .next() // move to the next list item
    .find('img') // find the image tag in the next list item
    .attr('src'); // grab the source attribute of the found
    → image tag
```

I cannot stress enough the importance of commenting your code well. Although I won't be commenting a lot of the code in the book for space reasons, you can expect to see a lot of commentary within the code samples on the Web site. My personal style is to use the double slash at the end of a line when the comment is quick and use larger comment blocks (beginning with /* and ending with */) when I need to be more descriptive.

```
// is a short comment
```

```
/* this comment may span multiple lines and can be very
→ descriptive */
```

Armed with this knowledge, you can traverse the DOM elements for this list. Given that you know the image source in the first list item, you can retrieve the source attribute from the second image in the list easily, like this:

```
var nextImage = $('img[src="bar.jpg"]') // define the starting point
    .closest('li') // travel up to the closest list item
    .next() // move to the next list item
    .find('img') // find the image tag in the next list item
    .attr('src'); // grab the sounrce attribute of the found
    → image tag
```

The variable nextImage now contains the value murkle.jpg.

LEARNING A FEW jQUERY TIPS

As I use and continue to learn more about the jQuery library, I've accumulated some good rules of thumb, including being specific about jQuery selectors, caching selectors, and packing up code to make it more efficient. These and other tips provided here will make your code more effective, provide you with some good tools, and shorten your development time.

SELECTING ELEMENTS SPECIFICALLY

To find the elements that you want to act on, jQuery has to traverse the DOM tree. Depending on the length and complexity of a page, the DOM can be quite large. Using grossly formed selectors can slow performance and lead to frustration.

jQuery reads selectors right to left, so if you have a selector like this:

```
$("div ul li a");
```

jQuery will gather all the anchors first, determine if they are within list items, and then find out if the list item is contained within an unordered list that is contained within a <div>.

Whew! It would be better to give one group of these items a class or an id attribute that will allow you to more directly identify one or more of the elements involved. For instance, the anchor tags in this group can be navigation elements and given a class of navigation (<a href="nav1.html" class="navigation">). That will allow you to shorten the selector to $(".navigation"). As an added bonus, the element can be more easily referred to and styled in CSS!

TIP: Thanks go out to the very supportive jQuery community for the tips included in this section. You can learn a lot by participating in the jQuery forums at http://forum.jquery.com. Forum participants are always willing to lend a hand to help you solve your jQuery and JavaScript problems.

MAKING QUICK WORK OF DOM TRAVERSAL

Sometimes, you might need to upgrade a poorly planned older site or application that was developed by someone else. The selector mentioned in the previous section, `$("div ul li a")`, might have to be used repeatedly to achieve the results that you are trying to apply with jQuery. If that is the case, you should cache the selector so that you only need to traverse the DOM once for that selector:

```
var myNavLinks = $("div ul li a"); // perform the traversal and
→  stores it

$(myNavLinks) // the new selector doesn't have to traverse the
→  tree again
```

Caching becomes a valuable performance tool when you want to manipulate dozens or maybe even hundreds of table rows and cells.

TROUBLESHOOTING WITH FIREBUG

Available for nearly every browser, Firebug is the leading tool for debugging and profiling JavaScript. It should definitely be in your Web development toolbox.

Firebug allows you to carry out several tasks, including watching your code "in action" to see how it behaves when events are triggered on your Web pages. For instance, in **Figure 1.4** a link has been clicked. If you look closely, you can see that several lines of HTML have been highlighted in yellow. Those lines are the portion of the HTML affected by the clicked link.

One of Firebug's handier features is its ability to identify JavaScript (and therefore jQuery) errors accurately, allowing you to quickly troubleshoot and correct problems.

I'll use some of Firebug's features throughout the book. To talk about and demonstrate all the features Firebug has to offer would take an entire book!

TIP: Firebug is a free download from http://getfirebug.com.

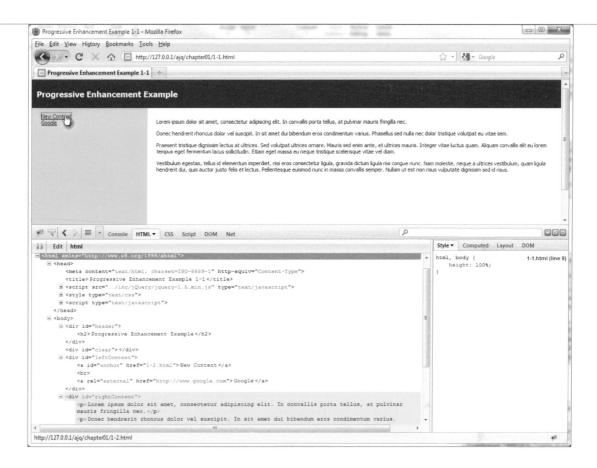

PACKING UP YOUR CODE

While you are working on writing your code, it helps to use lots of white space and comments. All of the comments and white space take up room, so it is best to pack up your code when you get ready to move your code into production. You may have noticed that the official jQuery site, as well as plugin developers, offer scripts in two versions: a normal version and a minified version. The minified version strips out most of the white space and comments. This ensures that your Web site is delivered more efficiently.

Several tools are available for packing up your code. One of my favorites is a freebie provided by Google, the Google Closure Compiler (http://code.google.com/closure/compiler). Google's Closure Compiler provides a quick method for minifying your code and offers some additional advantages like checking for illegal JavaScript.

FIGURE 1.4 Using Firebug, you can examine jQuery's actions.

For fun, let's pack some code in the file *spritenav.js*, which you will use later in the book. With white space and comments, the code looks like this:

```
/*
 * NAME: SpriteNav(jQuery)
 * AUTHOR: Jay Blanchard
 * DATE: 2011-01-10
 * BUSINESS RULE:    <if applicable>
 *
 * REVISION:    a20110110jb
 * STATUS:      open
 * USAGE:       call from web interface page

 *
 * REVISION HISTORY
 *
 * a20110110jb  - create CSS and XHTML for initial testing layout
 *
 */
$(document).ready(function() {

$(function() {
    /* set original values */
    $("#spriteNav span").css("opacity", "0");
    $("#spriteNav span.selected").css("opacity", "1");

    /* how do we hover? let me count the ways... */
    $("#spriteNav span").hover(function() {
        if($(this).attr("class").length == 0) {
            $(this).stop().animate({
```

```
              opacity: 1
          }, 75); // end mousein
      } else {
          $(this).css("opacity", "1"); // end mousein
      }; //end if
  }, function(){
      if($(this).attr("class").length == 0) {
          $(this).stop().animate({
              opacity: 0
          }, 250); // end mouseout
      } else {
          $(this).css("opacity", "1"); // end mouseout
      }; //end if
}); // end hover function


    /* click me! click me! */
      $("#spriteNav span").click(function() {
          /* we clicked, so remove the selected class from all */
          $("#spriteNav span").removeClass("selected");
          /* then add it to the selected one */
          $(this).addClass("selected");
          /* then fade out the previously selected item */
          /* be specific about the ones to be faded out */
          $("#spriteNav span:not(.selected)").stop().animate({
              opacity: 0
          }, 500);
      }); // end click function
  }); // end function
}); // end document ready function
```

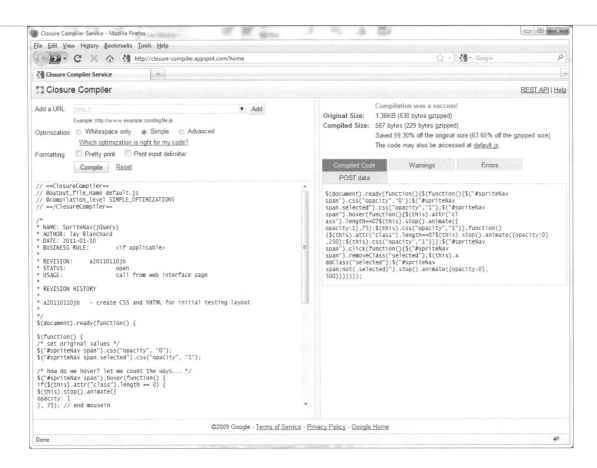

FIGURE 1.5 The code before and then after packing, which also reveals warnings and errors that are encountered by the Closure Compiler.

In **Figure 1.5** you can see the side-by-side comparison of the code before and after packing. After packing the code with the Google Closure Compiler, it becomes:

```
$(document).ready(function(){$(function(){$("#spriteNav span").css
  ("opacity","0");$("#spriteNav span.selected").css("opacity",
  "1");$("#spriteNav span").hover(function(){if($(this).attr
  ("class").length==0){$(this).stop().animate({opacity:1},75)}
  else{$(this).css("opacity","1")}},function(){if($(this).
  attr("class").length==0){$(this).stop().animate({opacity:0},
  250)}else{$(this).css("opacity","1")}});$("#spriteNav span").
  click(function(){$("#spriteNav span").removeClass("selected");
  $(this).addClass("selected");$("#spriteNav span:not(.selected)").
  stop().animate({opacity:0},500)})})});
```

Reduced to 40 percent of its original size (1360 bytes originally; 567 bytes after minifying), the code is very compact.

Although this is a good example of the gains to be made while minifying jQuery code, you really don't need to minify small files. If you are using a number of small files, it is best to combine them and then run them through the reduction process. If you plan to minify your files, be sure to keep one copy that you use for editing with all the white space and comments intact, and then minify when you are ready to use the file on a production Web site or application.

USING RETURN FALSE

Anyone who has done any amount of JavaScript programming, including programming with jQuery, has run into `return false;`. For the most part, many have used it improperly. Let's look at an example, an HTML anchor tag link:

```
<div><a href="inc/content.html">Click Here!</a></div>
```

Typically, you might apply something similar to the following jQuery to handle the anchor tag:

```
$("div a").click(function() {
    var link = $(this).attr("href");
    $("#content").load(link);
    return false;
});
```

In this example you want to be able to click the link and have that link not perform as it normally would; you want it to just load the information from the link into the element with an `id` of `content`. So, you insert `return false;` into the function. It works! But do you really know how?

Because `return false` works so well, you may not realize when it trips you up later on. The `return false` function first calls `preventDefault();` and then it calls `stopPropogation()`. The function `stopPropogation()` stops the *click* event in this case from bubbling up the DOM, which may prevent subsequent *click* events from working on the ancestors you may add later. You'll end up scratching your head a lot when your seemingly perfect code fails to do what you ask of it with no errors lurking about to give you a clue as to what happened.

More often than not what you should use is preventDefault(), as shown in the following highlighted code:

```
$("div a").click(function(e) {
    var link = $(this).attr("href");
    $("#content").load(link);
    e.preventDefault();
});
```

Take a few minutes to become familiar with the other related functions, stopPropogation() and stopImmediatePropogation(), because you may find them handy and revealing!

FIDDLING WITH jQUERY CODE

One of the most useful and coolest tools I've seen in many years is a Web application called jsFiddle (http://jsFiddle.net). Developed by Piotr Zalewa as "a playground for Web developers," jsFiddle is a great Web site where you can combine HTML and CSS while experimenting on that code with jQuery (**Figure 1.6**). The tool supports several different versions of jQuery and is an excellent troubleshooting tool.

Using the jsFiddle Web site is a great way to share code with other developers for discussion, troubleshooting, or bragging rights. The Web site also allows you to include the latest jQuery UI (user interface) code in your experiments.

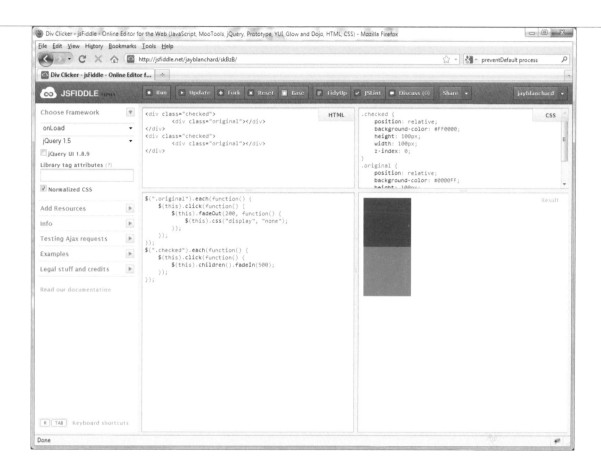

FIGURE 1.6 Using jsFiddle, you can test a jQuery code snippet.

COMBINING jQUERY
WITH OTHER CODE

Throughout the book, you'll be using several technologies to bring your Web applications to life. To start, you'll use HTML, CSS, and JavaScript, and then mix in PHP and MySQL to support further interaction.

STARTING WITH HTML

HTML is what you'll use to start all of your Web pages. Use of the latest version of HTML, HTML5, is on the rise, and examples in the book use it where appropriate. Because HTML5 is still in development, browser support is limited. I recommend plenty of cross-browser testing when using HTML5.

jQuery can select HTML DOM elements easily. For instance, if you have a form input element:

```
<input name="username" type="text" size="48" />
```

you can use the jQuery selector $('input[name="username"]') to interact with the element.

STYLING WEB PAGES WITH CSS

CSS can be tricky territory because different browsers provide different levels of support for the properties that CSS has to offer. Cross-browser testing is still required to make sure that what displays in one also displays in another. It is very important to understand that it is OK if your sites do not look exactly the same from browser to browser.

jQuery will support the latest and greatest CSS version, CSS3, and all of its properties, but make sure that you test in many browsers because that is the only way you can determine if what you see is acceptable to you.

USING PHP AND MYSQL

As one of the most popular server-side languages on the Web, PHP has made its mark on the technology you know and use every day. For the examples and projects in this book, you'll be using PHP not only for supporting asynchronous data requests to the server (AJAX), but also for shortening your development time with jQuery.

You will couple PHP with the MySQL database to support and enhance your jQuery projects.

Keep in mind that you can use any number of languages and database products with jQuery in the ways that I will present in the book—the choice is totally up to you.

PROGRESSIVE ENHANCEMENT

In 2003, Steve Champeon, speaking at the very popular SXSW Interactive conference in Austin, Texas, coined the term *progressive enhancement*. The concept arrived at just about the same time as some earlier JavaScript libraries.

The process behind progressive enhancement is to first develop your markup, then add style to that markup (CSS), and finally bring into play enhanced interaction via JavaScript.

In the good old days of Web development, designers and coders were stuck with a paradigm called *graceful degradation*. Everyone designed their sites for the latest browsers using the latest technologies and then "fixed" their pages by inserting hacks or removing JavaScript functionality so that they would gracefully degrade and be usable by older, less-capable browsers or in situations where the user might have JavaScript disabled. Developers attempted to perform browser detection using JavaScript so that they could deliver flashy interaction in every browser available. It was tiresome and frustrating. Steve Champeon's concept changed all of that.

There is a better way to describe progressive enhancement. In his 2008 article, "Understanding Progressive Enhancement" (www.alistapart.com/articles/understandingprogressiveenhancement), on the A List Apart Web site, Aaron Gustafson painted my favorite picture of what progressive enhancement is when he wrote, "If you're a candy fan, think of it as a Peanut M&M: Start with your content peanut, marked up in rich, semantic (X)HTML. Coat that content with a layer of rich, creamy CSS. Finally, add JavaScript as the hard candy shell to make a wonderfully tasty treat (and keep it from melting in your hands)."

Let's examine a quick example of progressive enhancement. Here is a portion of *1-1.html* (available in the code download at www.appliedjquery.com in the folder *chap1/1-1.html*):

```
<body>
    <div id="header"><h2>Progressive Enhancement Example</h2></div>
    <div id="clear"></div>
    <div id="leftContent">
        <a href="1-2.html" id="anchor" >New Content</a><br />
        <a href="http://www.google.com" rel="external">Google</a>
    </div>
    <div id="rightContent"></div>
</body>
```

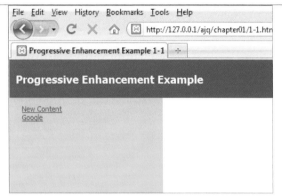

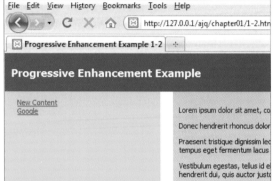

FIGURE 1.7 The basic progressive enhancement page with HTML and CSS only.

FIGURE 1.8 The result of clicking the New Content link in *1-2.html*.

The markup is pretty standard. Adding some basic CSS produces what you see in **Figure 1.7**.

I've also produced the HTML and CSS for a second page called *1-2.html*, which is in the folder *chap1/1-2.html*. If you click the link for New Content, that page will load normally (**Figure 1.8**). The only change made, other than adding some content for this example, is in the CSS that causes the content to be displayed in a burnt orange box:

```
#rightContent {
    width: 75%;
    margin-left: 20px;
    padding-top: 10px;
    padding-left: 10px;
    background-color: #FFCC66;
    vertical-align: top;
    float: left;
}
```

The site works perfectly, even though it is rather bland. Let's add just a bit of jQuery without touching any of the current markup.

1. Include the jQuery library by placing a tag in the <head> section of *1-1.html*:

```
<head>
    <meta http-equiv="Content-Type" content="text/html;
    ⇢ charset=ISO-8859-1" />
    <title>Progressive Enhancement Example 1-1</title>
    <script type="text/javascript" src="../inc/jQuery/8
jquery-1.5.min.js"></script>
```

2. Add a code block also within the <head> tags, although it is not necessary to do so, as you will see in later examples:

```
<script type="text/javascript">
$(document).ready(function(e) {
    $("#anchor").click(function() {
        $("#rightContent").load("1-2.html #rightContent > p");
        e.preventDefault();
    });
});
</script>
```

Basically, the code specifies, *Anytime the element identified as anchor is clicked, load the paragraphs from 1-2.html file's rightContent area into 1-1. html file's content area.*

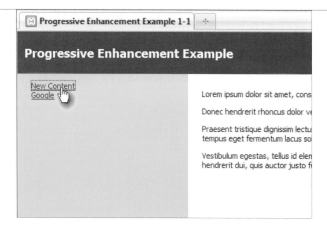

FIGURE 1.9 The content from the second page appears without the distracting background color.

Now when you click the New Content link, the page does not reload and the content appears as you expect, without the yucky background color (**Figure 1.9**).

Adding jQuery without using inline JavaScript tags is known as *unobtrusive JavaScript* and adheres to the principles of progressive enhancement. None of the HTML tags had to be changed, and if JavaScript is disabled, the pages will continue to work as designed. No more embedding JavaScript calls within the HTML tags!

In addition, the CSS here is unobtrusive, too. There are no style attributes as part of the HTML tags, but jQuery does give you the ability to change styling on the fly by giving you ways to add and remove classes and directly manipulate the CSS of every element on the page. You'll be using these functions frequently throughout the book.

PLANNING **DESIGN** AND **INTERACTION**

Any good Web application begins on paper, perhaps with a few basic sketches. By the end of the book, you'll have the ability to greatly enhance your sites with jQuery, so planning is especially important. You don't want to just throw jQuery code willy-nilly into your Web pages without a plan, or soon you'll have interaction overload. So many page elements will change and move on the screen that you'll get your visitor's attention, but not in the ways that you want to gain that attention.

Creating a storyboard is a great way to plan how you will guide the visitor through your site. Drawing a storyboard doesn't require any special skill. You can use sticky notes, sketches, flowcharts, or even the UML (Unified Modeling Language) to show how potential interactions behave and pages connect to each other. Be sure to ask lots of "what ifs." What if the viewer clicks here? What if the mouse scrolls over this section of the page? What if the total is over $100? What if you put your spinning, flaming logo right in the center of the page?

Asking questions like these and creating a basic layout of the site will open your eyes to how your visitors will see and interact with your Web pages. It will also give you some ideas for how you can build more jQuery widgets that add value to your sites.

WRAPPING **UP**

In this chapter, you learned about the jQuery JavaScript library, how to write the proper syntax for jQuery, and how jQuery selectors are like CSS selectors. You learned how jQuery interacts with the DOM and how you can use jQuery to traverse the DOM. You gained knowledge of tools like Firebug, jsFiddle, and the Google Closure Compiler to help you troubleshoot, test, and make your jQuery scripts ready for use on live Web sites and applications. Finally, you learned how to combine jQuery with HTML, CSS, and other languages using Progressive Enhancement techniques to keep all of your code and scripts compartmentalized for easy maintenance and to let site visitors with less-capable browsers use your content with restriction.

Now that you are armed with some good tools and an understanding of the jQuery basics, it is time to jump right in. To learn how jQuery can interact with the browser and events associated with the browser, just turn the page!

2

WORKING WITH EVENTS

The bread and butter of jQuery is its ability to interact with all kinds of browser and physical events, including mouse movement, form interaction, and keyboard events. You can take control of these events using jQuery to provide your Web-site visitors with a much richer interactive experience.

By binding events such as a mouse click or a keypress to text, links, images, and other DOM elements, you can call into action myriad functions from animation to AJAX. Functions can be combined to create complex chain reactions, a very cool thing.

In this chapter I'll show you how to gain control over many of these events while creating a fictional Web site called Photographer's Exchange. You will combine the events to create effects that will make your Web audience sit up and take notice. Other events are very subtle and will add flavor to your Web applications.

FIGURE 2.1 The front page of Photographer's Exchange. The text is used as a place-holder for development you will add later.

You will design the Photographer's Exchange Web site to allow photographers to show off their pictures and techniques. Users will be able to upload pictures and edit information about those pictures. Additionally, users will be able to submit articles about photography. Visitors will be able to search the site using different criteria. The front page of the site will showcase featured photographs and articles from photographers. **Figure 2.1** shows the basic layout of the site ready for editing.

NOTE: All of the code in this book is available as a download from the book's Web site at www.appliedjquery.com/download.

MAKING NAVIGATION GRACEFUL

If you want to apply the principles of progressive enhancement—as discussed in Chapter 1—to your site, you need to make your navigation as graceful as possible. The easiest way to do this is to fully form your links as if JavaScript, and therefore jQuery, is not available for your visitors.

Open the *chap2/2-1.php* file. You'll find an unordered HTML list containing three links:

```
<a href="search.php" rel="searchWindow" class="modal"
→ id="search"><span>Search</span></a>

<a href="register.php" rel="registerWindow" class="modal"
→ id="register"><span>Register</span></a>

<a href="login.php" rel="loginWindow" class="modal"
→ id="login"><span>Login</span></a>
```

Each link works properly in the absence of JavaScript. Clicking on any of them causes the respective page to be loaded into the browser.

> **NOTE:** To save time and space in this book, I did not create the additional Web pages. The content for each modal window, which is contained in 1-1.php, can be placed in separate pages if you are concerned that users will not have JavaScript available.

This set of links will be used to call modal windows into the browser.

CREATING AND CALLING MODAL WINDOWS

Modal windows are a clever way for users to interact with Web sites and applications. They provide smooth transitions by placing content "above" the current Web page and can give users information, as well as receive information from users either in forms or a confirmation dialog. Once the modal window is closed, users return to the same content in the Web browser that they were viewing previously.

Each modal window is used to perform a specific action in the site: search, register, or login. You do not have to make any modifications to the HTML for the links; all you have to do is add the proper jQuery.

1. Create a jQuery statement that selects all of the anchor tags that have a class of modal:

   ```
   $('a.modal').click(function() {
   ```

You have now handed over control of the click event to jQuery or have bound jQuery's click event to the anchor tag. This binding allows jQuery to handle the click event and any functions assigned to that event.

The remainder of the function decides which modal window to open, where to place the window, and how to close the modal window. Additionally, the function places a semitransparent "shade" over the entire site to make the modal window stand out. You can find the complete code in *chap2/inc/jqpe.js* under the section commented /* modal windows */.

2. Store the value of the rel attribute from the currently clicked item in a variable that will be used later in the function:

   ```
   var modalID = $(this).attr('rel');
   ```

3. Fade in the modal window that you selected and add a link that allows you to close the modal window. A graphic element (*close_button.png*) is used to make the close button look nice:

   ```
   $('#' + modalID).fadeIn().prepend('<a href="#"
   → class="close"><img src="grfx/close_button.png"
   → class="close_button" title="Close Window"alt=
   → "Close" /></a>');
   ```

   In the file *chap2/inc/modal.css*, the margins and padding were defined for each of the modal windows. To get them to center on the screen, you need to account for the extra space created by the padding and margins so that the proper offset can be applied. In this case there is a 20-pixel margin and 20 pixels of padding surrounding each modal window. That means that you must add 80 pixels to the height and width. With the height and width set, you then divide by 2 to get the proper margin.

4. Assign the horizontal and vertical margin calculated values to the variables modalMarginTop and modalMarginLeft:

   ```
   var modalMarginTop = ($('#' + modalID).height() + 80) / 2;
   var modalMarginLeft = ($('#' + modalID).width() + 80) / 2;
   ```

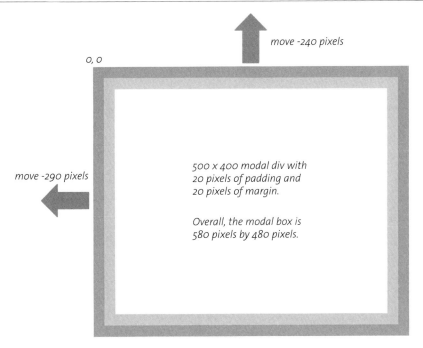

move -240 pixels

0, 0

move -290 pixels

500 x 400 modal div with
20 pixels of padding and
20 pixels of margin.

Overall, the modal box is
580 pixels by 480 pixels.

FIGURE 2.2 The modal window box, including padding and margins. The top-left corner of the modal window is located at 50 percent of the window height and width to begin. Setting the top and left margins with negative numbers moves the modal box to the center of the browser window.

5. Now add the margin information to the modal window's CSS to center it:

```
$('#' + modalID).css({
    'margin-top' : -modalMarginTop,
    'margin-left' : -modalMarginLeft
});
```

Figure 2.2 shows a model of the modal box and how much it must be offset to the top and left of the browser window to center the box.

If you don't calculate where the center of the box should go, the upper-left corner of the box will be centered in the browser window, as shown in **Figure 2.3**.

FIGURE 2.3 The modal box without calculating where the center of the box should go. The top-left corner of the modal box is at 0, 0 for the browser window's 50 percent height and width.

SIZING UP **ANIMATIONS**

When creating the modal window, you invoked the very first animation using the jQuery method `fadeIn()`. jQuery has a number of built-in animation methods, including `fadeIn` and `slideDown` as well as the `animate` method that allows you to create custom animations.

What is an animation?

In jQuery an animation is the act of moving an element from one CSS state to another CSS state smoothly. Animation can only be used on CSS rules that have numerical properties. jQuery uses a set of algorithms to calculate each of the points from the start of one state to the end of another state. A simple example is opacity.

If an element is invisible, its opacity is 0. To make the element fully visible, you set its opacity to 1. Depending on the length of time assigned to the transition, jQuery will calculate discrete steps needed to make the element appear to fade in (or out), moving opacity from 0 to 1 or vice versa.

jQuery also supports queues so that you can combine animations to create complex movements and changes.

The jQuery user interface (UI) extends jQuery basic animation events and adds several additional effect methods, including color animations.

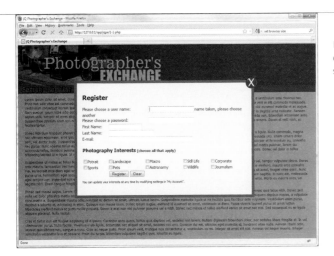

FIGURE 2.4 The modal window for registration is opened and is properly centered with the shaded, see-through background.

CREATING A SHADED BACKGROUND

The last order of business for opening the modal window is creating a shaded background. The shade is actually a semitransparent div through which you can still see the Web site. It is a very cool effect and helps users to understand that they are still on your site but that their attention should be focused on the content highlighted for them. You'll use a similar version of the see-through div for other widgets in the Web site.

1. Append a new div to the body to make the shade:

    ```
    $('body').append('<div id="modalShade"></div>');
    ```

2. Animate the shaded background to partial opacity to make it somewhat transparent:

    ```
    $('#modalShade').css('opacity', 0.7).fadeIn();
    ```

3. Close the click function with the return false; method to keep the link from trying to load another page into the browser.

    ```
    return false;
    });
    ```

Once complete, the jQuery code opens the modal window in the center of the browser window with a shaded background that allows users to see the Web page beneath it (**Figure 2.4**).

CONTROLLING THE FUTURE WITH LIVE() AND DELEGATE()

jQuery provides two methods for binding events to elements created now or in the future: live and delegate. Both save you the additional work of adding new event bindings as you add new elements dynamically. The primary difference between the two is that live does not support DOM traversal, whereas delegate will support binding of events to specific DOM elements.

To use live, you must use it immediately after a selector to bind to an event, just as you did in the code for closing the modal window:

```
$('a.close, #modalShade').live('click', function() {...
```

On the other hand, delegate can be used as follows:

```
$('ul#myList').delegate('li', 'click', function() {...
```

This binds the click event to each of the list items (<li>) now and in the future. If you append more list items to the unordered list, they will all have the click function bound to them.

Don't worry about handling form information or processing that information right now. I'll cover form handling and processing in Chapter 3, "Making Forms Pop" and Chapter 4, "Being Effective with AJAX."

CLOSING THE MODAL WINDOW

Users must be able to close the window and get rid of the shade, so you need to give users a way to get back to the Web site.

1. Start the close function by binding the close graphic and modal shade to a jQuery click method:

   ```
   $('a.close, #modalShade').live('click', function() {
   ```

   Neither of these elements existed in the DOM (see Chapter 1 for a short discussion of the DOM) originally, so you have to use a special jQuery function, live, to bind the click to these elements.

2. Determine which modal window to close by getting the `id` of the parent of `a.close`:

```
var thisModalID = $('a.close').parent().attr('id');
```

3. Now fade out the modal window and the shade. When the fade-out is complete, use the callback function `fadeOut` provides to remove the `div` that held the shade and the link that was prepended to the modal window:

```
$('#modalShade, #'+thisModalID).fadeOut(function() {
    $('#modalShade, a.close').remove();
});
return false;
});
```

In simple terms a *callback* is a block of executable code that is passed as an argument to another function. The block of code in the callback will run when the original function is complete. You issue a callback to the `fadeOut` function as highlighted:

```
$('#modalShade, #'+thisModalID).fadeOut(function() {
    $('#modalShade, a.close').remove();
});
```

The fade-out completes before issuing the callback to remove the `#modal-Shade` and `a.close` element from the DOM.

Combining multiple jQuery methods in this way makes a click on a link a pretty powerful event. Can you bind the `click` event, or any other event, to elements that are not links? Of course you can, and you already have. Look at the following line again:

```
$('a.close, #modalShade').live('click', function() {
```

The highlighted value is the `id` for the `div` that held the shade, which is also bound to the `live` `click` function. This allows users to click anywhere on the shade to fade out the modal window and perform the other items in the function. Binding to nonlink-type elements is common when using jQuery.

BINDING EVENTS TO OTHER ELEMENTS

jQuery gives you the flexibility to bind events to any element available in the DOM. This gives you the capability to set up highly interactive user interfaces. Creating a truly fun and intuitive user experience is easier than ever because you are not limiting your users to just clicking a link or a button on your Web site.

The Photographer's Exchange Web site needs a way to feature members' photographs. A simple photo carousel will provide an excellent method of showcasing the members' talents while allowing you, as the developer, to flex your creative muscles.

BUILDING AN IMAGE CAROUSEL

Let's add a simple version of a photo carousel to the site now.

The concept for the carousel is very simple and is based on an unordered list of thumbnail images. You can see this list added to the site in *chap2/2-2.php*:

```
<div id="carouselContainer">
    <div id="carouselOuter">
        <div id="scrollLeft"><img src="photos/arrowLeft.jpg" /></div>
        <div id="carouselInner">
            <ul id="carouselUL">
            <li><img class="carThumb" src="photos/thumb_ka1.jpg" /></li>
            <li><img class="carThumb" src="photos/thumb_ka2.jpg" /></li>
            <li><img class="carThumb" src="photos/thumb_ka3.jpg" /></li>
            <li><img class="carThumb" src="photos/thumb_ka4.jpg" /></li>
            <li><img class="carThumb" src="photos/thumb_ka11.jpg" /></li>
            <li><img class="carThumb" src="photos/thumb_ka12.jpg" /></li>
            <li><img class="carThumb" src="photos/thumb_ka13.jpg" /></li>
            <li><img class="carThumb" src="photos/thumb_ka14.jpg" /></li>
            </ul>
        </div>
        <div id="scrollRight"><img src="photos/arrowRight.jpg" /></div>
    </div>
</div>
```

Now that you have a list of images, you need to add the following carousel features:

- Automatic scrolling.

- Scrolling that stops when a mouse cursor hovers over any portion of the carousel.

- Scrolling that continues when the mouse cursor is not hovering over any portion of the carousel.

- Highlighting an image when the mouse cursor hovers over a thumbnail of that image.

- Controlling manual scrolling.

- Displaying a larger version of a picture when its respective thumbnail is clicked.

Before you can start adding these features, you need to create the container for the carousel using CSS. Let's cover that first.

SETTING UP THE CAROUSEL CSS

To make the carousel effect work well, it must have a solid container. The container will be defined by the CSS along with the markup that you created earlier.

1. Set up the #carouselInner rule to allow only a certain number of thumbnails to be visible at any one time:

```
#carouselInner {
    float: left;
    width: 510px;
    overflow: hidden;
    background: #000000;
}
```

The #carouselInner rule sets up a visible area of 510 pixels. Anything outside of the element assigned to this rule will not be visible. The 510-pixel area is calculated by adding the widths of three thumbnails (160 pixels each) plus 10 pixels for each thumbnail. The additional pixels allow for padding around each image.

2. Create a left margin that allows two images to be hidden off to the left of the carousel. Setting this margin is the most important part of the #carouselUL rule. Having two images to the left of the carousel ensures that the scrolling will happen smoothly. Make sure that the whole carousel is wide enough to hold the number of thumbnails you plan to display. In this case #carouselUL is designed to hold a maximum of 50 thumbnails:

```
#carouselUL {
    position: relative;
    list-style-type: none;
    left: -340px;
    margin: 0px;
    padding: 0px;
    width: 8500px;
    padding-bottom: 10px;
}
```

3. Now set the height and width of the list items:

```
#carouselUL li{
    float: left;
    width: 160px;
    height: 128px;
    padding: 0px;
    background: #000000;
    margin-top: 10px;
    margin-bottom: 10px;
    margin-left: 5px;
    margin-right: 5px;
    text-align: center;
}
```

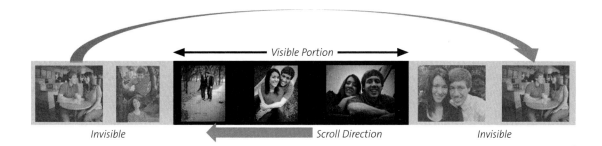

Figure 2.5 gives you an idea of how list items will be moved. As the carousel scrolls to the left, the first list item is moved to the end of the list while the item is invisible. The reverse happens (the last list item is moved to the first spot) when the carousel scrolls to the right. The user gets the impression that the images are on a carousel going around and around.

Once the style information has been defined, you can begin working on adding the features to the carousel using jQuery.

FIGURE 2.5 The visible and invisible portions of the carousel. You can also see how the images will move to make the carousel "infinite." The thumbnails will start over at the beginning of the list when the last one is displayed.

NOTE: There is much more to the CSS (chap4/css/carousel.css) for the carousel, but it is mostly decorative or setting up space for the arrows that will be used for manual control of the carousel. Additionally, the style information for the modal window to display the larger pictures is defined.

ADDING AUTOMATIC SCROLLING

It is time for you to start adding the features defined for the carousel. You'll first create a function that automatically scrolls the carousel. Create a file called *carousel. js* and save it in the *chap2/inc* folder.

1. Create the function using the function keyword and call the function autoCarousel. Then set the variable itemWidth equal to the width of one of the list items in the carousel and add 10 to it to make space for the padding:

```
function autoCarousel() {
    var itemWidth = $('#carouselUL li').outerWidth() + 10;
```

2. Determine how far to the left the carousel needs to move. Recall that the left margin of the CSS was set to -340 originally, so the moveFactor will be -510. Assign the results of that calculation to the variable moveFactor:

```
var moveFactor = parseInt($('#carouselUL').css('left'))
    → - itemWidth;
```

3. Now the fun really begins! Bind the animate method to the unordered list identified by #carouselUL. Then the list of images is moved to the left so that the images' left margins are the same as the moveFactor. Add the duration of slow and easing transition of linear for tighter control of the animation:

```
$('#carouselUL').animate(

    {'left' : moveFactor}, 'slow', 'linear',
    → function(){
```

4. Move the first list item to the end of the list, after the last list item. This line of code, contained in the animation's callback function, contains the secret to making the carousel infinite:

```
$("#carouselUL li:last").after($("#carouselUL
    → li:first"));
```

By moving the list item and changing the order of the HTML list as a whole, you can make the pictures appear to keep going around the carousel.

TIP: Easing, in jQuery terms, tells an animation how fast to move at different points during the animation's progress. jQuery includes two default easing methods: *linear* and *swing*. *Linear* moves the animation steadily from point A to point B with no speed change. *Swing* moves the animation slowly at first, faster near its midpoint, and then slows down as it reaches its end. Both of these easing methods will help to smooth animations, making them less jerky. You can create some cool effects by using George Smith's jQuery Easing Plugin. The plugin makes dozens of additional easing types available to use in your jQuery applications. The plugin is available from the GSGD Web site at http://gsgd.co.uk/sandbox/jquery/easing.

5. Close out the function by resetting the left margin back to its original value and closing all of the brackets and braces:

```
    $('#carouselUL').css({'left' : '-340px'});
  });
};
```

If you don't reset the left margin, the carousel will continue to scroll to the left, and eventually the pictures will be out of sight.

6. Call the autoCarousel function by placing it in a setInterval function. Give the setInterval method an identifier by assigning it to a variable. Set the interval to 2000 milliseconds (2 seconds):

```
var moveCarousel = setInterval(autoCarousel, 2000);
```

Now you can load the page. You'll see that the carousel starts automatically and pauses for 2 seconds between each animation.

7. Use the very next line of code to make all the thumbnails and the arrow graphics appear to be faded:

```
$('.carThumb, #scrollLeft, #scrollRight').css({opacity: 0.5});
```

You'll take advantage of the opacity being set to a faded state when you create the hover functions.

ADDING THE HOVER FUNCTIONS

You'll bind the hover function to the thumbnail images identified by the class of carThumb as well as the divs containing the arrows that will be used to manually control the scrolling of the carousel. Three actions are required for the hover function:

- Stop the scrolling when a mouse cursor hovers over any portion of the carousel.

- Highlight the image when the mouse cursor hovers over a thumbnail.

- Continue scrolling when the mouse cursor is not hovering over any portion of the carousel.

um dolor sit amet, consectetur adipiscing elit. Sed a sollicitudin nibh. Aliquam lacinia feugiat felis sed malesuada. Fusce accumsan laoreet eros, a vestibulum a
velit vitae est commodo commodo vel quis dui. Cras iaculis vehicula malesuada. Nulla ut velit sed purus blandit ultrices vel quis risus. Sed lacinia velit in elit co
. Vestibulum consequat laoreet ipsum, at blandit orci aliquam et. Aenean sit amet mauris non sapien euismod adipiscing ac luctus nisi. Curabitur id nulla et ni
t ac augue. Nam suscipit ipsum vitae odio condimentum ultricies. Ut pretium turpis ut odio sagittis non fringilla nulla varius. Integer scelerisque sapien eu eros
stie. Aenean sapien velit, semper sit amet aliquet non, volutpat vulputate ante. Lorem ipsum dolor sit amet, consectetur adipiscing elit. In orci elit, aliquet vitae

FIGURE 2.6 The mouse cursor over one of the images in the carousel. The image has been faded to full opacity, and the carousel has stopped scrolling.

1. Bind the hover function to the class carThumb and elements with an id of scrollLeft and scrollRight:

   ```
   $('.carThumb, #scrollLeft, #scrollRight').hover(function() {
   ```

   The hover function consists of two sections, one for *mouseover* and one for *mouseout*. The jQuery hover method combines this functionality to give you a tremendous amount of flexibility.

2. Bind the jQuery stop and animate methods for the *mouseover* portion of the function to elements represented by $(this). The stop makes sure that the current animation will quit when you move the mouse away or perform some other action. Without stop, the animations would continue to queue up and run, and that is not desirable for the hover function:

   ```
   $(this).stop().animate({
       opacity: 1
   }, 75);
   ```

   The animation makes the image fade to full opacity very quickly (75 milliseconds). This gives the appearance of the image being highlighted and fulfills one of the requirements. The cursor is hovered over a thumbnail in **Figure 2.6**, making it appear to be brighter than the thumbnails adjacent to it.

3. Stop the scrolling animation of the carousel by clearing the `setInterval` function. Identify the interval to be cleared by passing the identifier moveCarousel to the `clearInterval` function:

```
clearInterval(moveCarousel);
```

4. Add the code to fade the image in the *mouseout* portion of the hover function:

```
}, function() {
    $(this).stop().animate({
        opacity: 0.5
    }, 250);
```

The *mouseout* side of the jQuery hover function reverses the fade of the opacity and does so more slowly (250 milliseconds) just for effect. Note that you did not apply any easing to either side of the hover function. Easing will work here, but the times for the movement to either full or half opacity are so fast that most easing methods would hardly be noticed.

5. Restart the carousel's automatic scrolling by calling the `setInterval` function in the last line of the *mouseout* side of the hover function:

```
moveCarousel = setInterval(autoCarousel, 2000);
});
```

The requirements for the carousel are being met pretty quickly. Next, you'll give the Web-site visitors a way to control the scrolling of the carousel manually.

CONTROLLING MANUAL SCROLLING

Web-site visitors need the ability to manually scroll the carousel so they can look for specific images. Adding manual control is fairly simple, even though the movement of the carousel may seem backwards compared to the image that is clicked. In other words, clicking the right arrow moves the carousel to the left, and clicking the left arrow moves the carousel to the right.

A portion of the functionality for manual control was completed for the automatic scroll function autoCarousel (the following highlighted code). All that you need to do is wrap the code in a function that binds a click function to the element identified as scrollRight:

```
$('#scrollRight').click(function(){
    var itemWidth = $('#carouselUL li').outerWidth() + 10;
    var moveFactor = parseInt($('#carouselUL').css('left')) - itemWidth;
    $('#carouselUL').animate(
        {'left' : moveFactor}, 'slow', 'linear', function(){
        $("#carouselUL li:last").after($("#carouselUL li:first"));
        $('#carouselUL').css({'left' : '-340px'});
    });
});
```

If you've been really observant, you'll notice that this click event is bound to an arrow image that points to the right but moves the carousel to the left. As mentioned earlier, the movement might seem a little backwards for these functions, but there is a very good reason.

Visitors to Web sites have been conditioned by actions that they have performed for most of their lives. One of the most prominent of these conditions is turning the page of a book or a newspaper. This action requires you to grasp a section of the page on your right and move it to the left. It seems quite natural that this movement will reveal new content the way you expect it to. The same goes for the carousel. Clicking on the right moves the carousel to the left and feels very natural. You can test this by making a couple of changes to the function.

Moving the carousel to the right requires only a couple of changes.

1. Make a copy of the function that was used to set up manual control when clicking on the right arrow, and paste the newly copied code below that function.

2. Change the first line of the function to bind the click function to the scrollLeft selector:

```
$('#scrollLeft').click(function(){
```

3. Change the calculation assigned to the moveFactor variable to add the itemWidth instead of subtracting it:

```
var itemWidth = $('#carouselUL li').outerWidth() + 10;
var moveFactor = parseInt($('#carouselUL').css('left')) +
→  itemWidth;
```

The distance moved by the carousel is the same as it was before; it is just moving in a different direction. This difference in direction is accomplished by animating the move from -340 pixels left to -170 pixels left (the carousel moves from -340 pixels left to -510 pixels left when animating to the left):

4. Create the function that binds the animate method to the carousel:

```
$('#carouselUL').animate(
    {'left' : moveFactor}, 'slow', 'linear', function(){
```

5. Move the last list item to a place before the first list item:

```
$("#carouselUL li:first").before($("#carouselUL
→  li:last"));
```

Making this move is the opposite of the action that was performed before to reorder the image list and makes the carousel "infinite" in the opposite direction if the user continues to manually select the scrollLeft option.

6. Reset the left margin to its original location with the last line of code to complete the requirement for manual control of the carousel:

```
$('#carouselUL').css({'left' : '-340px'});
    });
});
```

FIGURE 2.7 The relationship between the standard left margin for the carousel, -340 pixels left, and the margins that get set temporarily to support the animation.

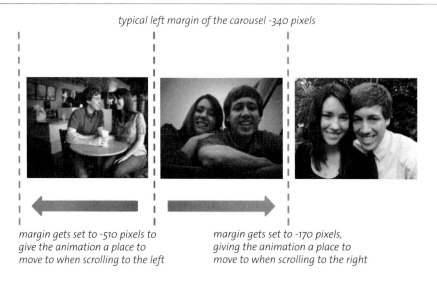

typical left margin of the carousel -340 pixels

margin gets set to -510 pixels to give the animation a place to move to when scrolling to the left

margin gets set to -170 pixels, giving the animation a place to move to when scrolling to the right

To understand the movement, **Figure 2.7** illustrates the normal left margin of the carousel at -340 pixels. The margin gets moved to the right or left temporarily as needed by the carousel click functions. This gives the animation method a "go-to" location.

NOTE: The style rule for the container that holds the arrows is included in chap2/css/carousel.css.

You need to add one more requirement to complete the carousel, and it is a huge one (excuse the pun). The carousel needs a method to display larger images.

ZOOMING IN ON LARGER IMAGES

When site visitors spot a thumbnail that they would like to get a better look at, you do not want them to just squint at the thumbnails and try to imagine them as larger images. By applying some CSS and jQuery, it is easy to give users a way to view larger pictures by clicking a thumbnail.

1. Using a technique similar to the creation of modal windows with form elements, create a div just before the closing body tag in *chap2/2-2.php*:

    ```
    <div id="photoModal" class="photoModal"></div>
    ```

2. Add the style rules for photoModal to *chap2/css/carousel.css*:

```
.photoModal {
    display: none;
    background: #FFFFFF;
    color: #000000;
    border: 20px solid #FFFFFF;
    float: left;
    font-size: 1.2em;
    position: fixed;
    width: auto;
    height: auto;
    top: 50%;
    left: 50%;
    z-index: 200;
}
```

It is important that you include a *height* and *width* property (highlighted) in the rule because these properties ensure that the image loaded into the *div* will fill the div properly and support the calculation that centers the picture within the browser window.

Next, you'll add the additional functions to handle the large images to the file you created earlier, *chap2/inc/carousel.js*. The first addition should be a function that loads all of the larger images into hidden divs having a class of photoHolder. It is necessary to load the images this way because jQuery cannot measure the height and width of something that is not yet loaded. Without the facility to measure elements not yet in the DOM, loading each image when the thumbnail is clicked may give you erratic results.

1. Bind the thumbnails with a class of carThumb to the each method to begin the function:

```
$('.carThumb').each(function(){
```

2. Extract the image's path and name information based on the source of the thumbnail. For example, the first line assigns *photos/thumb_ka1.jpg* to the variable photoInfo:

```
var photoInfo = $(this).attr("src");
```

3. Split the thumbnail path information apart at the forward slash:

```
var photoPathArr = photoInfo.split('/');
```

The split creates an array called photoPathArr. This array contains two pieces of information; *photos* contained in photoPathArr[0] and *thumb_ka1.jpg* in photoPathArr[1].

4. Concatenate a forward slash to *photos* (contained in photoPathArr[0]). The forward slash is needed to truly represent the path for the images:

```
var photoPath = photoPathArr[0]+'/';
```

5. Perform another split to get the actual name of the full-sized image:

```
var photoInfoArr = photoInfo.split('_');
```

The name of the full-sized image will be contained in photoInfoArr[1].

6. Reassemble the two pieces to provide the path to the full-sized image like *photos/ka1.jpg*:

```
var photoSrc = photoPath+photoInfoArr[1];
```

Note that manipulating text as you just did occurs frequently in jQuery (and other programming languages). As a matter of fact, you'll see similar text manipulation later in this function when you bind the click event to the thumbnails. As your skills grow, you'll be able to write functions that will process text manipulations like this quickly, and more important, as snippets of code that are reusable.

7. Define the images by creating a new image with the $('<img/>') selector and bind the image to the load function:

```
$('<img/>').load(function(){
```

8. Append a div to the body of the HTML document to hold the full-sized image:

```
$('body').append('<div class="photoHolder"><a
⇢ href="'+photoSrc+'"</div>');
```

9. Set the CSS display property to none for each of the elements assigned the class photoHolder. This is to make sure that each newly added element is invisible to the Web-site visitor:

```
$('.photoHolder').css('display','none');
```

10. Give the new $('<img/>') its source information:

```
}).attr('src', photoSrc);
});
```

As the each function loops through the unordered list of images, each full-sized image will be placed into its respective element and hidden away from the user.

For the click function that will be bound to the thumbnails, you will go through the same text-manipulation steps that were performed for the image-loading function. The steps are repeated again because the load and click functions are discrete from each other and cannot access each other's variables.

1. Bind the elements having a class of carThumb to jQuery's click method:

```
$('.carThumb').click(function() {
```

2. Step through the text-manipulation steps to get the path and full-sized image name:

```
var photoInfo = $(this).attr("src");
var photoPathArr = photoInfo.split('/');
var photoPath = photoPathArr[0]+'/';
var photoInfoArr = photoInfo.split('_');
```

3. Create an image tag for the full-sized photograph:

```
var photoImgTag = '<img src="'+photoPath+photoInfoArr[1]+'"
⇢ id="currentPhoto" />';
```

4. Get the name of the modal window to be used from the `rel` attribute of the thumbnail:

```
var modalID = $(this).attr('rel');
```

5. Place the image tag into the modal window:

```
$('#' + modalID).html(photoImgTag);
```

6. Apply the fade to the *photoModal* to make it appear in the browser window. Additionally, append a button that allows visitors to close the window to the modal window:

```
$('#' + modalID).fadeIn('slow', 'swing').append('<div
→ class="photoNote"><a href="#" class="closePhoto"><img
→ src="grfx/photoClose.jpg" class="closeX"
→ title="Close Photo" alt="Close" /></a></div>');
```

7. Load the current height of the HTML *body* into the variable bodyHeight:

```
var bodyHeight = $('body').height();
```
```
$('#currentPhoto').css('height', (bodyHeight - 200));
```

The bodyHeight variable is then used to set the total height of the enlarged image. Doing this will keep the enlarged image within the boundaries of the browser window, preventing the site visitor from having to scroll up and down to see the full image. The height applied to the enlarged image is 200 pixels less than the total height of the browser window, which will also allow for a nice-looking border around the picture.

TIP: Name items carefully so that their information is reusable in ways that will shorten your code and allow you to write more efficient functions. Prefixing the photograph's name with "thumb_" in this case will give you all the information you need to create the proper path for retrieving the full-sized images. The function for uploading photos (in Chapter 3) will name the thumbnails and full-sized images for you.

FIGURE 2.8 The finished product. A larger version of a thumbnail photo has been loaded into the browser window for all to enjoy.

8. Use the same calculation that centered the modal windows earlier to center the current modal window:

```
var modalMarginTop = ($('#' + modalID).height() + 40) / 2;
var modalMarginLeft = ($('#' + modalID).width() + 40) / 2;
$('#' + modalID).css({
    'margin-top' : -modalMarginTop,
    'margin-left' : -modalMarginLeft
});
```

9. Close out the function by adding the see-through shade to the background to make the photograph stand out:

```
$('body').append('<div id="carouselShade"></div>');
$('#carouselShade').css('opacity', 0.7).fadeIn();
return false;
});
```

Clicking a thumbnail now reveals a larger photograph centered in the browser window (**Figure 2.8**).

FIGURE 2.9 The primary
navigation sprite is pretty
basic, but you can achieve
spectacular results with the
technique.

FIGURE 2.9 The primary navigation sprite is pretty basic, but you can achieve spectacular results with the technique.

The function to close the modal window containing the photograph is the same function that was created in the section "Creating and Calling Modal Windows."

Binding events to elements is an exciting tool for making your Web applications come to life. The ability to combine jQuery events, such as click, hover, fade, and animate, provides a wealth of opportunities to create highly interactive experiences for your Web-site visitors.

One of the most popular interactive opportunities to come along has its roots in old-school game design—using sprites.

CREATING SPRITE-BASED NAVIGATION

Video games have been all the rage for the past 30 or so years, and anyone who has played early versions of games, such as Mario Brothers or Legend of Zelda, has played a game that used sprites as its basis for animation.

Simply put, a *sprite* is a graphic that describes multiple items, each item being at a specific location within the graphic. Each of the items in the sprite can be accessed by its location relative to a certain point in the sprite. Typically, the top-left corner (often described as 0, 0) of the sprite is the point used as the reference to each item's relative location.

The CSS layout is extremely important to the success of sprite-based navigation. The style sheet rules hold all of the location information for the items contained in the sprite. **Figure 2.9** shows the sprite used on the Photographer's Exchange site. This sprite consists of six items divided into two rows of three items each. The rows and columns are only used to keep the items in the sprite organized; elements can be anywhere you want them to be in a sprite. This sprite will be used for popping up several of the site's modal dialog windows.

The *mainNav.jpg* sprite (located in the *chap2/grfx* folder in the Web site's code) is divided into two categories. The first category contains the items in their natural state with no hover. The second category (the second line of items) is the group that shows a user has hovered over them with a mouse cursor.

FIGURE 2.10 The measurement for the sprite *mainNav.jpg*. This sprite is arranged in rows and columns, making identification of sprite elements very easy.

Determining the measurements of the sprite is critical. You'll use this measurement information in the CSS to define the location of items. Obtain the width of each column (for instance, the Search column) and the height of each row. **Figure 2.10** illustrates the measurements for the navigation sprite .

Note that the columns may have different widths; the height is consistent from row to row and must be for the animation effect to work properly.

> **NOTE:** In a sprite intended to be used as navigation on the side of the page (vertically), the column widths must be consistent from column to column but the heights may differ.

DEFINING THE MARKUP

The HTML markup for the navigation is quite simple, consisting of an unordered HTML list in *chap2/2-2.php*. Each list item contains an anchor tag and a span tag:

```
<ul id="spriteNav">
    <li><a href="search.php" rel="searchWindow" class="modal"
    ⇢ id="search"><span>Search</span></a></li>

    <li><a href="register.php" rel="registerWindow" class="modal"
    ⇢ id="register"><span>Register</span></a></li>

    <li><a href="login.php" rel="loginWindow" class="modal"
    ⇢ id="login"><span>Login</span></a></li>
</ul>
```

Although the markup is incredibly simple, the CSS is much more involved but not complicated. Each of the image's states must be described in the style sheet. These states also include the location information for each image.

CREATING CSS FOR SPRITES

Let's dig into the CSS (*chap2/css/spritenav.css*) now. First up in the style sheet is the basic housekeeping.

1. Define the height of the sprite in the spriteNav rule:

```css
#spriteNav {
    height: 30px;
    list-style: none;
    margin: 0;
    padding: 0;
}
```

2. Set each list item to float left so that each item will be side by side:

```css
#spriteNav li {
    float: left;
}
```

3. Define the background image for the list item anchor tags:

```css
#spriteNav li a {
    background: url(../grfx/mainNav.jpg) no-repeat;
    display: block;
    height: 30px;
    position: relative;
}
```

4. Now define the background image for the span tags nested in each list item anchor tag:

```css
#spriteNav li a span {
    background: url(../grfx/mainNav.jpg) no-repeat;
    display: block;
    position: absolute;
```

```
        top: 0;

        left: 0;

        height: 30px;

        width: 100%;

    }
```

The sprite is set as the background image for both the anchor links and the spans. This is the basis for how the whole highlighting effect works as you fade from one sprite to the other:

Each column of items must have a width and a position. The position is defined with *x* and *y* coordinates. Because you are working with the first row of items, the y-axis will be 0 for each item. The x-axis for each item is defined as the total width of all of the items that precede the one the mouse cursor is currently hovering over.

Look at Figure 2.10 again. In the sprite, the Search item in the top row has starting coordinates of 0 for the x-axis and 0 for the y-axis. The Search is 100 pixels wide, so the Register item still has a 0 y-axis, but the x-axis is -100 pixels. The Register item is 115 pixels wide, so the x-axis value for the Login item is the width of the Search item plus the width of the Register item, -215 pixels.

1. Define each list element's width and background-position:

```
    #spriteNav li a#search {

        width: 100px;

    }

    #spriteNav li a#register {

        width: 110px;

        background-position: -100px 0px;

    }

    #spriteNav li a#login {

        width: 90px;

        background-position: -215px 0px;

    }
```

2. Now define each span element's background-position:

```
#spriteNav li a#search span {
    background-position: 0px -30px;
}
#spriteNav li a#register span {
    background-position: -100px -30px;
}
#spriteNav li a#login span {
    background-position: -215px -30px;
}
```

Why use negative numbers? Imagine that each list element is a box and that the upper-left corner of that box is defined by the coordinates 0, 0. To get each item of the sprite to line up with the left edge of its list item, the sprite item must be offset to the left by the appropriate number of pixels.

For the sprite items in the second row, the sprite is not only offset to the left, it is offset upwards the necessary amount in a similar fashion.

Now that the CSS is properly defined, you can turn your attention to creating the jQuery that will animate the transformations of the sprite.

ADDING JQUERY ANIMATION

You could just use the HTML and CSS to create an immediate change from one sprite item to another, but what fun would that be? It's time to add some jQuery to give a smooth animated effect to the sprite's transitions.

1. Create the function and start by making sure that the spriteNav spans are set to default states:

```
$(function() {
    $("#spriteNav span").css("opacity", "0");
    $("#spriteNav span").text('');
```

Note that the span element is made invisible by reducing its opacity to 0. The span elements contain the sprite items that will be shown when the mouse cursor hovers over the span.

2. Bind the span elements to the jQuery hover method and set up the *mouseover* and *mouseout* portions of the function:

```
$("#spriteNav span").hover(function() {
        $(this).stop().animate({
    opacity: 1
    }, 100);
}, function(){
    $(this).stop().animate({
        opacity: 0
    }, 500);
});
});
```

FIGURE 2.11 The span has gained full visibility through the animation of the sprite's opacity.

You've seen the hover effect before as part of the requirement for the carousel. The difference here is that the hover method fades in the portion of the sprite that is described by #spriteNav span. Under normal circumstances, the span is totally transparent, allowing you to see the sprite item described by #spriteNav li. When the mouse cursor enters the span's space, the opacity of the sprite element is animated to being fully visible. **Figure 2.11** shows the hover effect, but I encourage you to load the code into a browser to get a full appreciation of the animation.

In Chapter 6, "Creating Application Interfaces," I'll show you how to create a more complicated interaction and animation with sprites.

WRAPPING **UP**

This chapter was packed with action based on binding Web-page elements to events such as click or hover. Once bound to an event, jQuery can perform any number of methods based on those events, including animation or appending new elements to the DOM. You moved smoothly from using a single event to combining events and methods to create widgets like modal windows, the infinite image carousel, and interactive sprite-based navigation.

This chapter has given you a solid baseline for using and combining events, but there are many more events you will want to explore as well. Let's take your jQuery development skills to the next level while exploring events you can use with forms.

3

MAKING
FORMS POP

Visitors to your Web site are not limited to interacting with basic events like clicks and hovers. You may want to give your users ways to provide information via fill-in-the-blank style forms. As a guardian of accurate data, you want to ensure that your users give you appropriate information by guiding them through the form-completion process (validation). As a designer, you want the form to be intuitive and easy to use. As a developer, you want to use the tools and events made available to you by jQuery to help your inner data guardian and designer create effective, high-quality forms.

In this chapter you'll work with the forms that have been developed for the Photographer's Exchange Web site and add jQuery's form events to enhance user interaction while validating the data the user is providing.

LEVERAGING **FORM EVENTS**

At first glance, the five events that jQuery exposes for form methods (blur, change, select, focus, and submit) seem to be rather paltry. Although the list appears short, combining these methods with other jQuery functions will yield a wide range of functionality.

To help guide your visitors along, you'll want to give them hints (or outright directions) on the next action you expect them to do. To keep Web-site users from just assuming they should enter information into a form, you can place the focus directly into the form element they should fill out first.

FOCUSING ON A FORM INPUT

One of the shortest and handiest jQuery methods is the focus function. Using this jQuery method, you can place the cursor right into the form element that you would like the user to fill out.

To use the focus function, it helps to know about the tabindex attribute of HTML elements, including anchor tags, form elements, and buttons. The tabindex defines the order (beginning with the lowest numbered item with a tabindex value) in which these elements should be selected based on clicking the Tab key on the computer's keyboard. You can set a tabindex value manually in each item like this:

```
<input type="text" name="penewuser" size="24" tabindex="0" />
```

In many circumstances, you'll have only one form per page, which will allow you to use the shortest form of the function:

```
$('input[tabindex="0"]').focus();
```

The selector chooses the form input that has a tabindex of 0 and places the cursor in that field.

This is simple enough, but what if there are multiple forms? That is the case in *chap3/3-1.php* of the Photographer's Exchange Web site. The three forms that users are expected to use the most are contained in hidden elements in the primary page of the site. Under normal circumstances, the first tabindex would likely be the first input in the first form. So how will you place the cursor into the first input of the form that is displayed?

Open *jqpe.js* and look for the comment /* focus on the first form element */. The next few lines contain the function that you'll use to identify the first input item in any of the forms that are opened in modal windows.

FIGURE 3.1 jQuery locates the first HTML Input Element object after the user clicks the Login element.

The opening move of the function is to look for all of the visible form inputs and start a loop through them:

```
$(':input:visible').each(function(i,e){
```

Because the forms start out with their CSS `display` property set to `none`, only the currently visible form elements will be looped through. The form becomes visible when its modal window is opened.

The each method contains a couple of extra variables: One identifies which form element is being worked with. The other is an iterator or counter that begins with 0. If you set an alert that fires on each loop (`alert(i+' '+e);`), it will show the counter and the form input object. **Figure 3.1** shows the alert.

The only line in the function assigns each visible form element's `tabindex` attribute a value, beginning with 1000:

```
  $(e).attr(1000, i);
});
```

The `tabindex` value is set high enough to avoid any other existing `tabindex` values that may exist in the Web page. When you apply the `focus` method to the form, you'll know that the cursor will end up in the first element of the form that you are currently displaying.

Once the visible form has properly assigned `tabindex` values, you can then use the focus method to place the cursor in the first input field:

```
$('input[tabindex="1000"]').focus();
```

The focus method as you have used it here actually causes the cursor to be placed on a certain element. You can also trigger an event when a user places focus on an element by tabbing to the element or selecting that element with a mouse click.

Now that you are focused, let's tackle something a little more challenging, validating email addresses with jQuery.

VALIDATING EMAIL ADDRESSES

Open *chap3/3-1.php* in your favorite text editor and locate the div with an id of registerForm. Within that form, you will find a line of HTML that describes the input for an email address:

```
<label class="label" for="email">Email: </label><input type="text"
    name="email" id="email" size="48" /><span class="error">please
    enter a valid email address</span><br />
```

The HTML error span is hidden normally, using a CSS rule (*chap3/css/modal.css*):

```
.error {
    display: none;
    color: #FF0000;
    font-size: 0.7em;
    margin: 0px 0px 0px 5px;
}
```

If there is an error performing basic email validation, the error span will be displayed by changing its display properties in the jQuery function designed to test the email address entered into the form.

Basic form validation does not use AJAX (I'll show you how to use AJAX to validate certain form elements in Chapter 4, "Being Effective with AJAX"). To get started with the jQuery email validation:

1. Open the *chap3/inc/jqpe.js* file. You will begin creating this function before the closing brackets of the document ready function wrapper.

2. Bind the blur method to the email input:

```
$('#email').blur(function() {
```

The blur method is engaged when tabbing or clicking away from the input element, causing the input to lose focus.

When the blur occurs, you'll need to employ a way to validate the email. One of the most powerful ways of performing a validation is by using a programming construct called a *regular expression*. I can hear the screams of horror now! The shrieking! The wailing!

However, once you understand regular expressions, there is really nothing to be afraid of. Regular expressions are a flexible way to match strings of text and are perfectly suited for performing the kind of matching needed to validate an email address. The regular expression used here breaks down quite easily.

3. Insert the regular expression designed to be a match for most email addresses and store that expression in the variable regexEmail:

```
var regexEmail = /^[a-zA-Z0-9._-]+@[a-zA-Z0-9.-]+
→ \.[a-zA-Z]{2,4}$/;
```

The first portion of the regular expression /^[a-zA-Z0-9._-]+ states that what is being matched should begin with alphanumeric characters and that the alphabetic characters can be either lowercase or uppercase. Periods, underscores, and hyphens are also allowed. The + sign indicates that this statement should match the preceding characters one or more times.

After the initial characters, there must be an @ sign, otherwise known as *at*.

After the *at* sign another set of alphanumeric characters, [a-zA-Z0-9.-]+, is allowed, along with periods and hyphens only. Next, a period, \., should exist to separate the domain and subdomain.

The regular expression ends with [a-zA-Z]{2,4}$. This indicates that the last portion of the item being matched must have only letters and can be from two to four characters in length. This is perfect for matching currently available Web domains.

4. Put the value of the form input element in the variable inputEmail:

```
var inputEmail = $(this).val();
```

5. Now let's test the value typed into the form against the regular expression using JavaScript's test method:

```
var resultEmail = regexEmail.test(inputEmail);
```

The test method returns true if the email address is valid or false if the address is invalid. This allows you to use a conditional test to determine if the error message should be displayed.

6. Create a conditional statement that will use the result of the regular expression test to determine whether or not the error message should be displayed for the user:

```
if(!resultEmail){
```

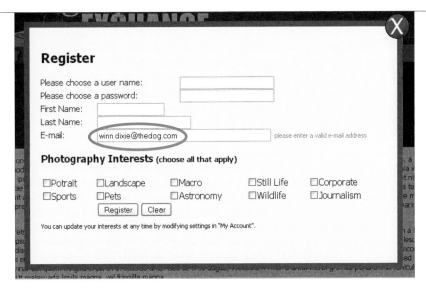

FIGURE 3.2 The user has left a space in the name. This is not valid when matched against the regular expression used for validating email addresses.

The exclamation point here essentially specifies: *If the condition of the variable is not true, the test has failed.*

7. If the test has failed, display the error next to this element (#email) by changing its CSS display properties:

   ```
   $(this).next('.error').css('display', 'inline');
   ```

8. If the test has succeeded, either the first time the user enters the information or when the user goes back and corrects the information, set the CSS display property of the error so that it does not show:

   ```
   } else {
       $(this).next('.error').css('display', 'none');
   }
   ```

9. Close out the jQuery email validation function with the proper braces and brackets:

   ```
   });
   ```

   When an incorrectly formatted email is entered, the error span is displayed when the blur event occurs, taking focus away from the email input area. The result is shown in **Figure 3.2**.

If you look closely at the code in *chap3/3-1.php*, you'll notice that there is more than one span element assigned the class error. Why don't all of these spans become visible when there is an error present? The answer lies in the method used in the conditional statement of the function. Look again at this line:

```
$(this).next('.error').css('display', 'inline');
```

The trick is in the .next() method. The jQuery object $(this) represents the object with an id of #email. One sibling of #email is #error. If you type the HTML in a hierarchical fashion, you can see the relationship more clearly:

```
<form name="register" id="registerForm" action="inc/peregister.php"
    method="post">
    /* other form elements */
    <label class="label" for="email">Email: </label>
    <input type="text" name="email" id="email" size="48" />
    <span class="error">please enter a valid email address</span>
    /* more form elements */
</form>
```

Each highlighted element is the child of the form element and a sibling to all of the elements at the same level within the markup. The next sibling for #email is just the error span immediately following it in the code. Using the next method will cause only this error span's properties to change so that it becomes visible.

Now let's combine the form change method with the next method to turn off an error once the form password field is filled in.

MAKING SURE AN INPUT IS COMPLETE

Making sure that a form field is not blank before submission is the most basic method of form input validation. There are several methods for creating functions that ensure that a field in an HTML form is filled out. You can force users to use certain characters with a regular expression, or you can make sure that the password meets a minimum length requirement.

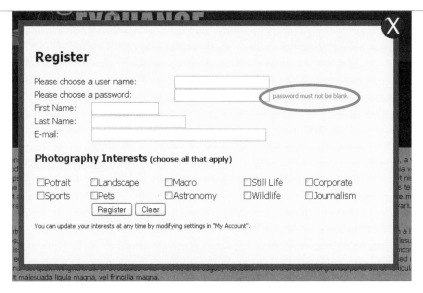

FIGURE 3.3 The user is warned against leaving the password field blank.

For the Photographer's Exchange Web site, the requirement is only that the password field not be left blank. The warning is displayed when the form is loaded, as shown in **Figure 3.3**.

1. Open *chap3/inc/jqpe.js* and begin by creating the function before the closing bracket of the document ready wrapper:

```
$(function() {
```

2. Get the length of the value contained in the form element having an id of penewpass. Store that length in a variable called passwordLength:

```
var passwordLength = $('#penewpass').val().length;
```

3. The first item in the code tests the length of the password field's value. If that length is zero, you display the warning:

```
if(passwordLength == 0){
    $('#penewpass').next('.error').css('display',
 →  'inline');
```

4. Set up the jQuery code to look for a change event occurring in the password input field. If a change occurs, the CSS method sets the error's display to none, which causes the warning message to disappear:

```
$('#penewpass').change(function() {
    $(this).next('.error').css('display', 'none');
});
```

5. Close out the braces and brackets for the function properly:

```
    }
});
```

Even though you are performing a lot of client-side data validation, you should always cleanse user-supplied data properly by removing potentially harmful syntax or even code statements entered into forms once that data reaches the server. Let's look at some of those cleansing techniques next as users are given a way to upload pictures to the Photographer's Exchange Web site.

FIGURE 3.4 The file upload form where site users will be able to upload up to five pictures at a time.

As you may already know, you cannot use AJAX to upload files. Preventing a client-side technology like AJAX from performing file uploads closes a potentially large security hole.

So how do you allow users to upload files to your Web site? In this section you'll learn a surefire (and secure) way to perform file uploads using an HTML *iframe* element and PHP while keeping the smooth interactivity you expect from jQuery.

To make the upload process effective and safe, you'll combine jQuery with PHP. Making sure that users upload the proper files is the first priority. The upload form that you'll use is in the file *chap3/3-4.php* and is illustrated in **Figure 3.4**.

PERFORMING CLIENT-SIDE VALIDATION

Because the site is for photographers, file uploads will be limited to *JPGs, JPEGs* (Joint Photographic Experts Group), and *PNGs* (Portable Network Graphics). These file types are especially suitable for digital photography. If the user selects any other file type, the upload form needs to prompt the user with a reminder. The HTML contains a hidden error span that will be shown if the file type selected is not correct:

```
<label class="label" for="pUpload1">Select File: </label><input
→ type="file" name="pUpload[]" id="pUpload1" value="" size="48"
→ /><span class="error">extension must be jpg, jpeg or png</span>
```

This is similar to the error messages applied in earlier forms. Place the jQuery code to catch the error in a file called pePhotoUp.js, which you will save in the *chap3/inc* folder.

1. Start the function by selecting the upload form's inputs and binding them to the each method:

```
$('input[name*="pUpload"]').each(function(){
```

The selector used is called an *attribute selector*. Attribute selectors allow you to specify one or more attributes and their respective values to filter a group of elements. Here the selector wraps all inputs whose name begins with pUpload.

2. Bind the inputs to the change method so that any change in the input field can be captured to trigger the balance of the function:

```
$(this).change(function(){
```

3. Set up a regular expression to test for the proper file-extension text. The function will then get the value of the changed input and test that value against the regular expression:

```
var regexPhotoExt = /\.(jpg|jpeg|png)$/i;
var photoName = $(this).val();
var resultPhoto = regexPhotoExt.test(photoName);
```

Let's dissect the regular expression used here. Working from right to left the i signifies that the test is case-insensitive. The dollar sign ($) ensures that the test is for the end of the string being tested. The meat of the expression (jpg|jpeg|png) is an array of three strings that are acceptable as a file extension. The period (escaped by a backslash) indicates that a successful test string will begin with a period. File extensions *.jpg*, *.jpeg*, or *.png* will pass the test.

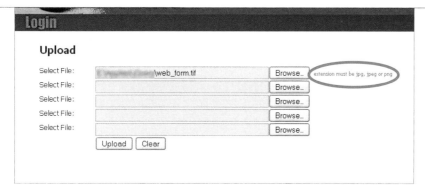

4. Create the conditional check that reveals or hides the error message:

```
if(!resultPhoto){
    $(this).next('.error').css('display', 'inline');
} else {
    $(this).next('.error').css('display', 'none');
}
    });
});
```

If the user chooses a file with an extension that does not match one of the values in the regular expression array, an error will be displayed, as shown in **Figure 3.5**.

> **NOTE:** A word of warning: Providing the user with a visual prompt does not actually prevent the file from being uploaded!

Life would be easy for designers and developers if all they had to do was provide a warning message to a Web-site visitor when that visitor tries to do something that the designer or developer doesn't want the visitor to do. The reality is that you must also validate the information when it gets to the server because some of your visitors may try to submit data or upload files that can do harm to your servers, or even worse, transmit virus-laden files to your other Web-site visitors. You'll learn how to validate that information next.

DEVELOPING SERVER-SIDE VALIDATION

Server-side validation in the Photographer's Exchange Web site is handled by a few lines of the PHP code during the file upload process. Let's isolate those lines to see how the validation is performed before moving on to creating the image upload function.

Locate the *photoUpload.php* file in the *chap3/inc* folder of the Photographer's Exchange Web site and open it. The file contains several different functions, but the focus in this section will be on the code used to validate uploaded files.

NOTE: PHP code will be used for all of the server-side processes in this book, but you can easily replicate these functions in any language.

Find the comment /* set up the file for validation */. The next few lines following this comment are the key to making sure that the file being uploaded is what it is supposed to be—an image file.

PHP sets up a temporary filename for the uploaded file. This temporary name is used by PHP to refer to the file until the upload is complete. The real name of the file is also available. These two names are saved to variables to make them easier to use:

```
$tmpName = $_FILES["pUpload"]["tmp_name"][$key];
$photoName = $_FILES["pUpload"]["name"][$key];
```

You'll see a familiar sight in the next line. The code is for the regular expression used for client-side validation; it is used because you should always validate user-supplied data, and jQuery did not prevent the user from clicking the Upload button even though an improper file type was chosen:

```
$regexFileExt = "/\.(jpg|jpeg|png)$/i";
```

The PHP function preg_match provides the same testing capability as JavaScript's test method:

```
if(preg_match($regexFileExt, $photoName)){
```

This level of testing may be good enough for some developers, but you really want to be safe. One way of adding an additional layer of testing in PHP is to use a function that will read the first few bytes of a file to determine the file's actual type. That function is `exif_imagetype`.

The `exif_imagetype` function can return over a dozen different constants, like `IMAGETYPE_JPEG`, when a test is valid. Users are allowed only two different file types on Photographer's Exchange (*jpg* and *jpeg* are the same from a binary standpoint), so two constants are placed into an array that will be used when testing:

```
$arrEXIFType = array(IMAGETYPE_JPEG, IMAGETYPE_PNG);
```

TIP: If you are using PHP, make sure that your version of PHP includes the EXIF (Exchange Image Information) extension. You will need that extension to use the EXIF functions.

The temporary file $tmpName is tested by the function `exif_imagetype`. Then the PHP function checks to see if the constant returned is in the array `$arrEXIFType`. If the constant matches one of the values in the array, the file upload is allowed to proceed:

```
if(in_array(exif_imagetype($tmpName), $arrEXIFType)){
    // perform the file upload
```

Now that the files can be validated properly, it is time to turn your attention to actually making the upload happen.

NOTE: The *exif_imagetype* returns the constant FALSE when the test fails.

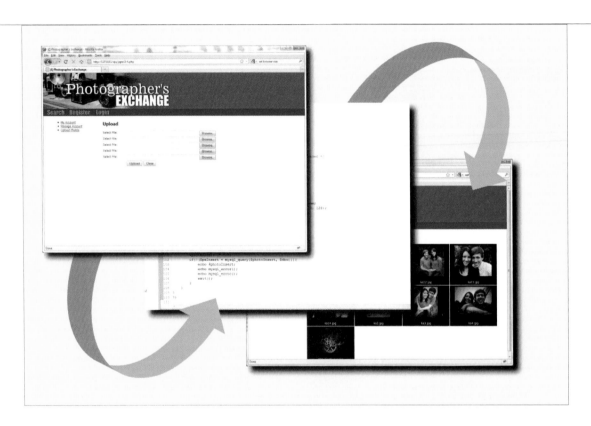

FIGURE 3.6 The path of a normal file upload begins on one Web page and ends on another Web page after the upload is processed.

UPLOADING FILES

Because AJAX cannot be used to upload files, you'll learn how to employ some jQuery magic to give the application the ability to move files from the user's computer to the Web site's server.

Normally, an upload form calls on the script that will process the file upload directly. Once the upload has been processed by the server, another Web page is loaded. **Figure 3.6** shows how the process begins with the form in a browser. The form sends the data to a script (in this case the PHP upload script) on the server for processing before redirecting the user to a new Web page.

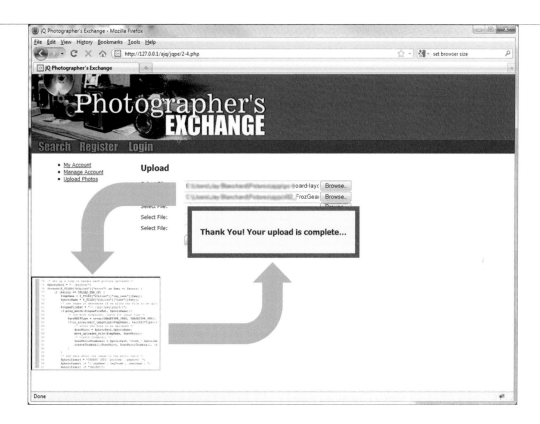

The new upload function uses a temporary and hidden HTML *iframe* that is called into existence by the jQuery function. Beginning the same way from a typical file upload form, the jQuery process then opens the *iframe* (shown for clarity in **Figure 3.7**) into which the PHP upload script is targeted. When the upload script is complete, the *iframe* is removed by the jQuery process and a modal window is presented to let the user know that the process has completed.

FIGURE 3.7 This screen reveals the magic behind the jQuery upload process. An *iframe* is temporarily created to hold the file-upload processing script.

SCRIPTING THE UPLOAD

The entire file upload process requires two parts, the PHP code that processes the uploaded files on the server side and the jQuery code that will be used on the client side by the Web browser. You'll create the client-side jQuery first.

1. Open the jQuery file *chap3/inc/pePhotoUp.js* in which you created the client-side file extension validation. Start the upload function immediately after the closing brackets for the file extension validation function. Bind the jQuery submit method to the upload form:

```
$(function(){
    $('#uploadForm').submit(function(){
```

2. Set up an *iframe* and append it to the Web-page's body. Set the *iframe's* display property to none; the user will never see it:

```
var iframeName = ('iframeUpload');
var iframeTemp = $('<iframe name="'+iframeName+'"
→ src="about:blank" />');
iframeTemp.css('display', 'none');
$('body').append(iframeTemp);
```

Now that the *iframe* is ready to use, the submit function provides the proper attributes to target the *iframe* with the PHP upload script. This is where the upload occurs.

3. Set up the attributes for the submit function to pass to the *iframe*:

```
$(this).attr({
    action: 'inc/photoUpload.php',
    method: 'post',
    enctype: 'multipart/form-data',
    encoding: 'multipart/form-data',
    target: iframeName
});
```

The image files are now uploaded to the server.

Let's put the finishing touches on the client-side portion of the file upload process. You do this by letting the user know the process has completed and performing some housecleaning duties, clearing the form and removing the *iframe*.

CREATING CALLBACK-STYLE FUNCTIONALITY

The last part of the jQuery upload script is placed into a short (1 second) setTimeout function. The timeout (you can experiment with the length of time allowed) allows several functions to take place without presenting jarring transitions to the Web-site visitor.

1. Create the setTimeout function:

    ```
    setTimeout(function(){
    ```

2. Remove the temporary iframe, because it is no longer needed:

    ```
    iframeTemp.remove();
    ```

3. Create a small function that will determine the length of the text in the input fields. The length information will be placed into the inputLength variable for use later in the file upload function:

    ```
    inputLength = 0;
    $('input[name*="pUpload"]').each(function() {
        inputLength += $(this).val().length;
    });
    ```

    You do not want to display the confirmation modal if the Upload button is accidentally clicked with no data in the input fields. To prevent accidental confirmation, a test is performed to make sure that inputLength is greater than zero.

4. Open a conditional statement that will check the value of the inputLength variable:

    ```
    if(0 < inputLength){
    ```

5. If the inputLength is greater than zero, append a div to the body that contains the confirmation message:

    ```
    $('body').append('<div id="ty" class="thankyouModal">
    ⟶  <h3>Thank You! Your upload is complete...
    ⟶  </h3></div>');
    ```

6. To ensure that the modal will be displayed in the center of the browser window, get the height and width of the div and then add the extra margin and padding width to it. This technique was used in Chapter 2 to center modal windows and photos from the carousel:

    ```
    var modalMarginTop = ($('#ty').height() + 60) / 2;
    var modalMarginLeft = ($('#ty').width() + 60) / 2;
    $('#ty').css({
        'margin-top' : -modalMarginTop,
        'margin-left' : -modalMarginLeft
    });
    ```

7. Fade in the confirmation message (**Figure 3.8**) so that the user knows the process has completed:

    ```
    $('.thankyouModal').fadeIn('slow', function(){
    ```

8. Clear the input fields so that the form is clean and ready to use again:

```
$('input[name*="pUpload"]').val('');
```

> **NOTE:** The message that is provided to the user in the file upload form only confirms that the process is complete. It does not confirm that the files have been sent to the server, nor does it report back errors. There are many ways to make this process much more robust. For example, you could modify the script to provide error messages or use AJAX to poll the directory that the files should be in.

9. Fade out the confirmation message slowly to give the site visitor a visual sense of action:

```
$(this).fadeOut(1500, function() {
```

10. Remove the confirmation modal from the DOM:

```
$(this).remove();
```

11. Make sure that all of the curly braces and parentheses are matched up and closed properly for the conditional statement:

```
            });
        });
    };
```

The time in milliseconds (1000 milliseconds equals 1 second) for the setTimeout function is placed prior to closing the function and then is followed by the remainder of the closing braces, parentheses, and semicolons:

```
}, 1000);});});});
```

> **TIP:** A good integrated development environment (IDE) editor will have bracket and parentheses matching built in.

When can the photos be displayed properly as full-sized images and as thumbnails? Let's turn to the PHP script that processes the uploaded files, *chap3/inc/ photoUpload.php*.

PROCESSING THE UPLOADED FILES

The PHP photo upload script does much more than just upload the files and validate them to ensure that your users are not sending malicious files to reside on your server. The script places the full-sized photos in the correct directory, creates properly sized thumbnails, and places data into the database corresponding to the files that are uploaded.

1. Create the connection to the MySQL database:

```
if(!$dbc = mysql_connect('localhost', 'username', 'password')){
    echo mysql_error() . "\n";
    exit();
}
```

NOTE: You will have to set up this connection with the server, user, and password information particular to your installation. Scripts for setting up various tables required by this application are in the chap3/sql directory of the code download available from www.appliedjquery.com.

2. You'll store all of the photos and thumbnails in a directory called (I racked my imagination over this) *photos*. The path to the directory is chap3/photos/. Assign that path to the $photoPath variable:

```
$photoPath = "../photos/";
```

3. Begin a loop to upload each image file and check if there is an upload error of any type. Files with errors will be ignored, but I strongly encourage you to look into methods for handling the errors and presenting information back to the user:

```
foreach($_FILES["pUpload"]["error"] as $key => $error) {
    if ($error == UPLOAD_ERR_OK) {
```

4. Add the next section of code, the validation code, which was explained earlier in this chapter:

```
$tmpName = $_FILES["pUpload"]["tmp_name"][$key];
$photoName = $_FILES["pUpload"]["name"][$key];
$regexFileExt = "/\.(jpg|jpeg|png)$/i";
if(preg_match($regexFileExt, $photoName)){
    $arrEXIFType = array(IMAGETYPE_JPEG, IMAGETYPE_PNG);
    if(in_array(exif_imagetype($tmpName), $arrEXIFType)){
```

5. Concatenate the photo's proposed path to the name that will actually refer to the image file, and then move the new image into its permanent directory file on the server:

```
$newPhoto = $photoPath.$photoName;
    move_uploaded_file($tmpName, $newPhoto);
```

At this point, the images have been uploaded, validated, named, and moved.

6. Transform the full-sized images into thumbnails that can be used in carousels and pages to allow users to edit information about the photos. Start by creating a path and name for the thumbnail:

```
$newPhotoThumbnail =
→ $photoPath.'thumb_'.$photoName;
```

7. Call the createThumbnail function (you will create the function in the section "Creating thumbnails" later in this chapter) and send the appropriate arguments to the function—the name of the full-sized photo, the name of the thumbnail that will be created, and the maximum width and height of the thumbnail:

```
createThumbnail($newPhoto,
→ $newPhotoThumbnail, 160, 128);
        }
    }
```

Before discussing the thumbnail creation function, let's finish this portion of the script, saving the data to the database.

SAVING IMAGE DATA

The photographers using the Web site will want to save and share information about their photographs with other users visiting the Web site. If you have run the SQL scripts to set up the database table for the photos, the table allows for some basic information about each photo: the image name, the name of the thumbnail, the user name of the person who uploaded the photo, and notes about the photograph.

During the upload process, three pieces of information are immediately available with which to populate the table.

NOTE: The user name is not really available at this point because registration and login has not been completed. These functions will be completed in Chapter 4, "Being Effective with AJAX." You'll want to modify SQL code after completing that chapter to account for the additions.

The SQL query to insert the image information is divided over several lines to increase readability and aid in troubleshooting when necessary. The query information should follow the file upload processing function in *chap3/inc/photoUpload.php*.

1. Declare the insert along with the database and table name:

   ```
   $photoInsert = "INSERT INTO `photoex`.`pephoto` ";
   ```

2. Declare the names of the columns that data will be entered into in the database table:

   ```
   $photoInsert .= "(`imgName`,`imgThumb`,`username`) ";
   ```

3. Insert into the table each of the values from the upload process:

   ```
   $photoInsert .= "VALUES(";
   $photoInsert .= "'".$photoName."', ";
   $photoInsert .= "'thumb_".$photoName."', ";
   $photoInsert .= "'' ";
   $photoInsert .= ")";
   ```

4. Close out the query and call PHP's mysql_query function to execute the query:

```
if(!($peInsert = mysql_query($photoInsert, $dbc))){
```

If there is an error with the query, several variables are printed out to the screen so that you can quickly and effectively troubleshoot the problem. Under normal circumstances, you would not want to reveal this information to your users. Instead, you would give the user a meaningful error message and log the results of the error variables so that you can examine them behind the scenes as part of the debugging process.

5. Set up the PHP variables that will provide troubleshooting information to you if something goes wrong with the database insert:

```
echo $photoInsert;
echo mysql_error();
echo mysql_errno();
exit();
```

6. Close out the PHP file upload function with the appropriate closing brackets:

```
        }
    }
}
```

With the photos safely uploaded and the data recorded in the database, the site is coming along well. One other addition you need to make is to ensure that thumbnails are created properly so they will work in the carousel included in the site earlier. Thumbnails will also be displayed in a tabular format when needed.

CREATING THUMBNAILS

In Chapter 2 you created an infinite carousel to display image thumbnails. To create thumbnails from all of the images uploaded, you'll use the PHP function described here.

When configuring the carousel, you determined that each image used could be no more than 160 pixels wide or 128 pixels tall. You need to send this information to the function along with a couple of other arguments. You'll use this line of code in the file upload function to call the thumbnail creation method into action:

```
createThumbnail($newPhoto, $newPhotoThumbnail, 160, 128);
```

thumb_cameras.jpg
160 pixels x 106 pixels

cameras.jpg
800 pixels x 533 pixels

FIGURE 3.9 Comparing the full-sized original with its much smaller thumbnail.

The following arguments are sent to the function:

- The name of the new photo in the variable $newPhoto.

- The name that you want the thumbnail to have in the variable $newPhotoThumbnail.

- The maximum width for the thumbnail in pixels.

- The maximum height for the thumbnail in pixels.

Keep in mind that the function will create any size thumbnail; all you need to do is change the last two arguments. As you will see, the function will calculate either the width or height as needed to make sure that the thumbnail is proportionally sized. **Figure 3.9** shows a thumbnail created by the process and how it retains its proportions compared to the original.

Let's dig in and create the PHP function in *chap3/inc/photoUpload.php* that will generate thumbnails from your images.

1. Start by declaring the function and its arguments:

```php
function createThumbnail($name, $filename, $newWidth, $newHeight){
```

2. Place the image's name into an array by *exploding* the variable. Using the example's name for the image, *cameras.jpg*, use the explode method to create an array ($arrPhotoName) with two entries, cameras and jpg. Use the next line to place jpg into the variable $fileExtPosition:

```php
$arrPhotoName = explode('.',$name);

$fileExtPosition = count($arrPhotoName) - 1;
```

PHP's explode method takes two arguments, one for the separator and one for the item to be *exploded*. The separator in this case is a period.

3. Depending on the image type (based on the file's extension), you call the appropriate PHP function to create a working image in the proper format. This working image will be used instead of the original image. Working with a copy of the image helps to ensure that nothing is done to destroy or ruin the original image:

```php
if (preg_match('/(jpg|jpeg)/i',
  → $arrPhotoName[$fileExtPosition])){

    $workingImg = imagecreatefromjpeg($name);

} elseif (preg_match('/(png)/i',
  → $arrPhotoName[$fileExtPosition])){

    $workingImg = imagecreatefrompng($name);

}
```

Note that regular expressions were used again. You must be getting used to them by now.

> **TIP:** The functions used to manipulate images in PHP for this function are supplied by the GD library, just one of the image manipulation libraries available for PHP. Make sure that your version of PHP is compiled with the GD library if you want to use the image manipulation functions used here.

4. Now the real fun of this function can begin. You need to get the width and height of the working image first. The following calculations will determine the new height and width for the thumbnail:

```
$oldX = imagesx($workingImg); // width
$oldY = imagesy($workingImg); // height
```

5. If the width of the working image is greater than its height, set the width to 160 pixels and calculate the number of pixels to make the height proportional:

```
if ($oldX > $oldY) {
    $thumbW = $newWidth;
    $thumbH = ($oldY * $newWidth) / $oldX;
}
```

6. If the height of the working image is greater than its width, set the height of the thumbnail to 128 pixels and calculate the number of pixels to make the width proportional:

```
if ($oldX < $oldY) {
    $thumbW = ($oldX * $newHeight) / $oldY;
    $thumbH = $newHeight;
}
```

7. For square images, you can set the height and width to the maximum height used in the carousel:

```
if($oldX == $oldY) {
    $thumbW = $newHeight;
    $thumbH = $newHeight;
}
```

8. Use PHP's ImageCreateTrueColor function and pass it the newly determined width and height for the thumbnail:

```
$newThumbnail = ImageCreateTrueColor($thumbW,$thumbH);
```

The thumbnail is now created.

> **NOTE:** The thumbnail creation function has been designed for simplicity's sake. The function works well with images that are typically proportioned within the maximum size ranges for the carousel. As image width and height values approach each other, but before the image becomes square, these simple algorithms will not keep the thumbnails within the maximum height and width range designed for the carousel. The way to correct this is to look at the calculated height and width of the thumbnail and adjust either the height or width again if either measurement falls outside of the range.

9. Resample the image to retain the quality of the thumbnail; you'll use PHP's imagecopyresampled to accomplish this. You must supply several arguments to this function for it to work properly:

- The destination image resource ($newThumbnail).

- The source image resource ($workingImage).

- The x and y coordinates of the destination point. This tells the resampling function which point to work from on the destination image. In this case it is the top-left corner of the image.

- The x and y coordinates of the source point. This tells the resampling function which point to work from in the source image. It starts in the top-left corner.

- The destination width and height.

- The source width and height.

```
imagecopyresampled($newThumbnail, $workingImg, 0, 0, 0, 0,
    $thumbW, $thumbH, $oldX, $oldY);
```

10. After resampling has occurred, move the image to its permanent home in the file structure of the Web site by outputting the file to the proper location. If the image is a *png*, you use PHP's imagepng to perform this action; if not, use imagejpeg:

```
if (preg_match("/(png)/i", $arrPhotoName[$fileExtPosition])) {
    imagepng($newThumbnail, $filename);
} else {
    imagejpeg($newThumbnail, $filename);
}
```

11. Destroy the resources to free up memory on the server:

```
imagedestroy($newThumbnail);
imagedestroy($workingImg);
}
```

Thumbnail creation is complete! By combining the jQuery upload process with PHP, you have created an effective way to allow users to upload files to your site. At the same time, you gain techniques for manipulating the files to suit your purposes and keep your server safe from harm.

Take the time now to upload some pictures and make changes to some of the form functions to get a good feel for how all of this works together. While you are doing this, think about ways that you can modify and improve this functionality for use in your forms.

WRAPPING **UP**

In this chapter you gained a firm grasp of working with forms and the data in those forms. You were introduced to methods such as employing regular expressions for validating data with jQuery in a form without a round trip to the server. Along the way you learned a couple of ways to provide meaningful user messages to the users of your forms. You also learned how to use jQuery (without AJAX) to upload files to your server via a hidden iframe element, along with methods of confirming the types of files you will allow your users to upload.

Just when you thought it was safe to get out of the form pool, you'll next learn how to use jQuery's AJAX methods. In Chapter 4, jQuery's AJAX functions are covered in depth to give you ways to improve and enhance your forms, and improve the user's experience by dynamically and smoothly loading content. Roll up your sleeves!

4

BEING **EFFECTIVE** WITH **AJAX**

AJAX, one of the hottest technology combinations to enter the Web development landscape in years, has fueled a surge in interactive Web design with its ability to load new content into an existing DOM structure.

jQuery simplifies using AJAX with several shorthand methods for the basic AJAX methods. For most developers and designers, these shorthand methods will be all that they ever need to use. The jQuery AJAX shorthand methods `post`, `get`, and `load` are featured in this chapter. jQuery also provides a robust feature set, including callbacks, for developers who want to customize their AJAX calls to provide richer interactive experiences. I'll show you how to use several of jQuery's AJAX features to enhance Web sites and applications. Let's start by completing the form validation that you started in Chapter 3.

Simply put, AJAX (Asynchronous JavaScript and XML) lets you use JavaScript to send and receive information from the server asynchronously without page redirection or refreshes. You can use AJAX to grab information and update the Web page that your user is currently viewing with that information. Complex requests can be made to databases operating in the background.

When new users register to use the Web site, they need to have unique user names. Their user name will be associated with other information, such as photos they upload or articles they write. It will be the key that lets them update information about the photos they submit.

Make sure that you first set up the database for the Web site by running the SQL file *chap4/sql/peuser.sql* on your database. Running this script in MySQL or any other database platform will create the Web-site's database, a user for that database, and the table that will be used to store Web-site visitor registration information. You can then start building the PHP file that will respond to the actions the AJAX functions will request.

BUILDING THE PHP REGISTRATION AND VALIDATION FILE

Photographers who want to share their images and perhaps write articles on photography will need a way to register information with the site that will allow them to log in and gain access to site features not accessible to nonregistered users.

You can create an interaction for this that will appear very slick to the user. With jQuery's AJAX functionality, you can avoid page reloads or redirections to other pages (**Figure 4.1**). The AJAX engine will send the requests to the PHP scripts on the server without disruption to the user experience.

Using PHP and jQuery, you'll create the functions that will support the registration interaction.

1. Open a new text file and save it as *chap4/inc/**peRegister.php***.

NOTE: If you'd like to use the PHP file provided in the download, feel free to skip ahead to "Setting Up the jQuery Validation and Registration Functions" section. Be sure to edit the PHP file with the proper user name, password, and host name for the database connection to match what you have set up on your database server.

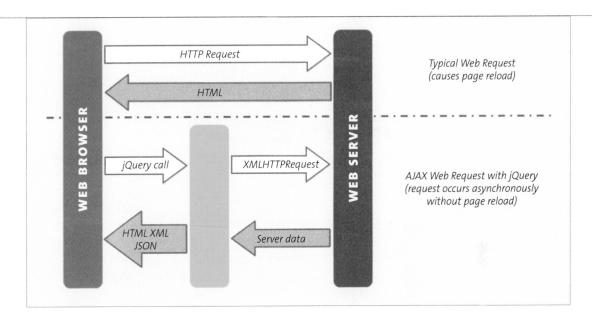

Typical Web Request
(causes page reload)

AJAX Web Request with jQuery
(request occurs asynchronously
without page reload)

2. Set up the database connection for the PHP function, including a method
   for returning errors if no connection can be made:

FIGURE 4.1
The difference between a typical HTTP request and the XMLHttpRequest utilized by jQuery's AJAX methods.

```php
if(!$dbc = mysql_connect('servername', 'username', 'password')){
    echo mysql_error() . "\n";
    exit();
}
```

Contained in this PHP file are three actions: one to complete registration,
one to validate the user name, and a method to allow registered users to
log in. The proper function will be called based on the name of the form
used in the AJAX function.

3. Use PHP's `switch` method to determine which form is submitted and set
   up the first case for the registration form:

```php
switch($_POST['formName']) {
    case 'register':
```

4. Check to see if the user name and password are set:

```php
if(isset($_POST['penewuser']) &&
→ isset($_POST['penewpass'])) {
```

5. If the user name and password are set, use the data from the form to complete a SQL statement that will insert the new user's information into the database:

```php
$peuserInsert = "INSERT INTO `photoex`.`peuser` ";

$peuserInsert .= "(`username`, `userpass`,
→ `userfirst`, `userlast`, `useremail`";
```

6. Because users can choose a number of photographic interests when they register, you must set up a loop to handle the check boxes that are selected in the registration form:

```php
if(isset($_POST['interests'])){
```

7. The loop used here counts the number of interests selected and properly formats the SQL statement to name those interests. Insert commas in the correct place, and close the initial statement with a closing parenthesis:

```php
$peuserInsert .= ",";
for($i = 0; $i < count($_POST['interests']);
    $i++){
    if($i == (count($_POST['interests'])
        - 1)){
            $peuserInsert .=
            "`".$_POST['interests'][$i]."`";
    } else {
            $peuserInsert .=
            "`".$_POST['interests'][$i]."`, ";
    }
}
$peuserInsert .=")";
```

8. Place the values from the registration form into the SQL statement in the correct order:

```
$peuserInsert .= "VALUES (";

$peuserInsert .= "'".$_POST['penewuser']."', ";

$peuserInsert .= "'".$_POST['penewpass']."', ";

$peuserInsert .= "'".$_POST['pefirstname']."', ";

$peuserInsert .= "'".$_POST['pelastname']."', ";

$peuserInsert .= "'".$_POST['email']."' ";
```

9. Inserting the correct values includes looping through any interests selected in the form and inserting the value "yes" for those interests:

```
if(isset($_POST['interests'])){

    $peuserInsert .= ",";

        for($i = 0; $i < count($_POST
          → ['interests']); $i++){

            if($i == (count($_POST['interests'])
              → - 1)){

                $peuserInsert .= "'yes'";

            } else {

                $peuserInsert .= "'yes', ";

            }

        }

}
```

10. Close the SQL statement properly:

```
$peuserInsert .=")";
```

If you were to print out the resulting SQL statement contained in the variable $peuserInsert, it would look something like this:

```
INSERT INTO `photoex`.`peuser`(`username`, `userpass`,
  → `userfirst`, `userlast`, `useremail`,`landscape`,
  → `astronomy`,`wildlife`) VALUES ('Bob.Johnson','ph0t0man',
  → 'Bob','Johnson','photoman@gmail.com','yes','yes','yes','yes')
```

11. Use the PHP function `mysql_query` to insert the data into the database, and the user will be registered:

```php
if(!($peuInsert = mysql_query($peuserInsert,
→ $dbc))){
    echo mysql_errno();
    exit();
}
```

CHECKING THE USER NAME FOR AVAILABILITY

Because the new user will typically fill out the user name first, the password and user name will not be set, so the `else` statement will be invoked. This is the PHP code that checks the user name to see if it exists in the database.

1. Create a SQL query that selects the user name typed into the registration form from the user database:

```php
} else {
$peCheckUser = "SELECT `username` ";
$peCheckUser .= "FROM `photoex`.`peuser` ";
$peCheckUser .= "WHERE `username` =
→ '".$_POST['penewuser']."' ";
if(!($peuCheck = mysql_query($peCheckUser, $dbc))){
    echo mysql_errno();
    exit();
}
```

If the name the user entered into the registration form is already in the database, the query will return a row count of 1. If the name is not in the database, the row count is 0.

2. Assign the count of the number of rows returned by the query to the database:

```php
$userCount = mysql_num_rows($peuCheck);
```

3. Echo the count value to be returned by the AJAX function for use by jQuery to determine if the user should enter a new user name in the registration form:

```
echo $userCount;
}
```

4. Complete the case statement for the registration form:

```
break;
```

CREATING THE PHP FOR USER LOGIN

After registering, the user can log in to the site and begin uploading photos and writing articles. Let's complete the login section of the PHP file.

1. Set up the case statement for the login code:

```
case 'login':
```

2. Check to see if the user name and password are set:

```
if(isset($_POST['pename']) && isset($_POST['pepass'])){
```

3. If they are set, send a query to the database with the user name and password information:

```
$peLoginQ = "SELECT `username`, `userpass` ";
$peLoginQ .= "FROM `photoex`.`peuser` ";
$peLoginQ .= "WHERE `username` = '".$_POST['pename']."' ";
$peLoginQ .= "AND `userpass` = '".$_POST['pepass']."' ";
if(!($peLogin = mysql_query($peLoginQ, $dbc))){
    echo mysql_errno();
    exit();
}
```

> **NOTE:** You should always make sure that data visitors enter into forms is cleansed by checking the data rigorously before submitting it to the database.

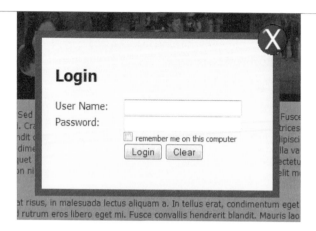

FIGURE 4.2 The check box a user can click to be remembered. The user will not have to log in again until the cookie associated with this action expires or is removed from the computer.

4. Set the variable $loginCount to the number of rows returned from the database query. If the user name and password are correct, this value will be 1:

```
$loginCount = mysql_num_rows($peLogin);
```

Next, you'll set up a cookie depending on the user's preference. A *cookie* is a small file that is placed on the visitor's computer that contains information relevant to a particular Web site. If the user wants to be remembered on the computer accessing the site, the user can select the check box shown in **Figure 4.2**.

5. If the login attempt is good, determine what information should be stored in the cookie:

```
if(1 == $loginCount){
```

6. Set up a cookie containing the user's name to expire one year from the current date if the "remember me" check box was selected:

```
if(isset($_POST['remember'])){
    $peCookieValue = $_POST['pename'];
    $peCookieExpire = time()+(60*60*24*365);
    $domain = ($_SERVER['HTTP_HOST'] !=
        'localhost') ? $_SERVER['HTTP_HOST'] :
        false;
```

The math for the time() function sets the expiration date for one year from the current date expressed in seconds, 31,536,000. A year is usually sufficient time for any cookie designed to remember the user. The information in the $domain variable ensures that the cookie will work on a *localhost* as well as any other proper domain.

7. Create the cookie and echo the $loginCount for AJAX to use:

```
setcookie('photoex', $peCookieValue,
  → $peCookieExpire,
'/', $domain, false);
        echo $loginCount;
```

8. Set a cookie to expire when the browser closes if the user has not selected the remember option:

```
} else {
        $peCookieValue = $_POST['pename'];

        $peCookieExpire = 0;

        $domain = ($_SERVER['HTTP_HOST'] !=
          → 'localhost') ? $_SERVER['HTTP_HOST'] :
          → false;

        setcookie('photoex', $peCookieValue,
          → $peCookieExpire,
'/', $domain, false);
        echo $loginCount;
}
```

9. Echo out the login count if the user name and password are not set. The value should be 0:

```
    } else {
        echo $loginCount;
    }
}
break;
```

NOTE: For more on PHP and how to use it effectively with MySQL, check out Larry Ullman's book, PHP 6 and MySQL 5 for Dynamic Web Sites: Visual QuickPro Guide (Peachpit, 2008).

With the PHP file ready to go, it is time to build the jQuery AJAX functions.

SETTING UP THE JQUERY VALIDATION AND REGISTRATION FUNCTIONS

Checking the new user name should be as seamless as possible for the registrant. The form should provide immediate feedback to users and prompt them to make changes to their information prior to the form being submitted. The form input (in *chap4/4-1.php*) element for the user name will be bound to the blur method:

```
<label class="labelLong" for="penewuser">Please choose a user name:
→ </label><input type="text" name="penewuser" id="penewuser"
→ size="24" /><span class="error">name taken, please choose
→ another</span>
```

1. Bind the form input for the user name to jQuery's blur method:

```
$('#penewuser').blur(function() {
```

2. Capture the value of the user name in the newName variable:

```
var newName = $(this).val();
```

Next, you'll validate with the post method.

1. Call the post method with the URL of the PHP script, data representing the name of the form that is being filled out, and the newName variable:

```
$.post('inc/peRegister.php', {
    formName: 'register',
    penewuser: newName
```

Note that the data passed by the post method is in name: value pairs. The value in each pair is quoted when sending the raw data. Variables such as newName do not need the quotes.

The results of calling the *inc/peRegister.php* script will automatically be stored for later processing in the data variable.

2. Define the callback for the post function and pass the data variable to the function, so that the results can be processed:

```
}, function(data){
```

The PHP function returns only the row count based on the query that was used to see if the user name was in the database.

3. Set up a variable to hold the information returned in the data variable:

```
var usernameCount = data;
```

4. Create a conditional statement that will display or hide the error message based on the data returned by the AJAX method. You'll recognize most of this conditional statement because it is similar to how validation error messages were delivered in Chapter 3:

```
if(1 == usernameCount){
    $('#penewuser').next('.error').css('display',
    → 'inline');
} else {
    $('#penewuser').next('.error').css('display',
    → 'none');
}
```

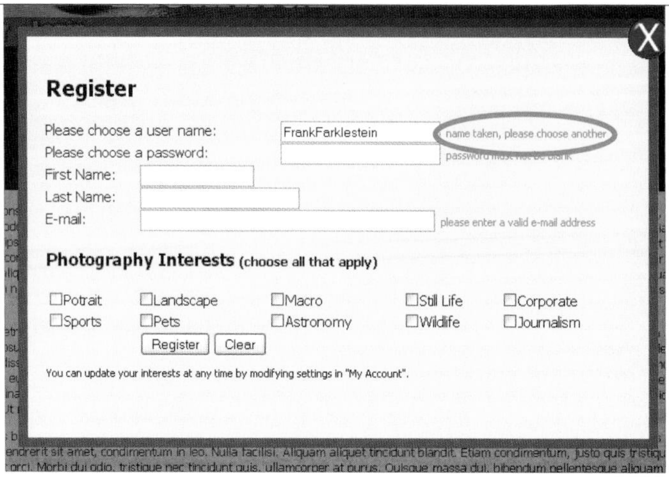

FIGURE 4.3 The user name FrankFarklestein is already in use by someone else. Who knew there were two of them?

5. Close out the post function by citing the data type you expect the server-side function to return:

```
    }, 'html');
});
```

If the PHP function returns a 1, the error span is displayed, as illustrated in **Figure 4.3**.

The registration function needs to submit the user's data or let the user know if there are still errors with the submission. If there are errors, the user needs to be prompted to fix the registration.

1. Start the registration function by binding the registration form to the submit method:

```
$('#registerForm').submit(function(e) {
```

The variable e holds information about the event object, in this case the submit event.

2. Because you will be using AJAX to submit the form, you do not want the submit event to perform as it normally would. To stop that from happening, you set the event to preventDefault:

```
    e.preventDefault();
```

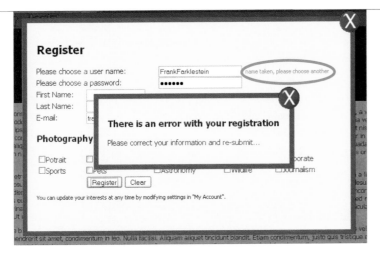

FIGURE 4.4 The modal prompt letting users know that they need to correct their registration information. In the background you can see that the user name is already taken; this must be changed.

3. Serialize the form data. The serializing creates a text string with standard URL-encoded notation. For most forms, this notation is in the form of key=value pairs:

```
var formData = $(this).serialize();
```

4. Now you can invoke the jQuery AJAX post method by providing the URL to post to and the serialized form data, and setting up a callback function:

```
$.post('inc/peRegister.php', formData, function(data) {
```

The PHP code will return 0 if the query to add the user is successful. If not, it will return a higher number, indicating that the user could not be added.

5. Store the information returned by the AJAX function in the mysqlErrorNum variable:

```
var mysqlErrorNum = data;
```

If an error is returned, you'll want to provide users with a prompt to let them know that they need to correct the information. The information is provided in a modal window as you have done before. **Figure 4.4** shows the modal window that you will set up next.

6. Test the value of the variable mysqlErrorNum to set up a conditional statement:

```
if(mysqlErrorNum > 0){
```

7. If `mysqlErrorNum` is greater than 0, append a modal window to the body of the Web page:

```
$('body').append('<div id="re"
→ class="errorModal"><h3>There is an error with
→ your registration</h3><p>Please correct your
→ information and re-submit...</div>');
```

8. Calculate and apply the margins for the new modal window just as you did before:

```
var modalMarginTop = ($('#re').height() + 60) / 2;
var modalMarginLeft = ($('#re').width() + 60) / 2;
$('#re').css({
    'margin-top' : -modalMarginTop,
    'margin-left' : -modalMarginLeft
});
```

9. Add the code that will fade in the modal window:

```
$('#re').fadeIn().prepend('<a href="#"
→ class="close_error"><img src=
→ "grfx/close_button.png" class="close_button"
→ title="Close Window" alt="Close" /></a>');
```

10. Provide a method to close the modal window containing the error warning:

```
$('a.close_error').live('click', function() {
    $('#re').fadeOut(function() {
        $('a.close_error, #re').remove();
    });
});
```

11. If no error was returned, fade out the registration window and clear the form:

```
        } else {
            $('#registerWindow, #modalShade').
          → fadeOut(function() {
                $('#registerForm input[input*="pe"]').val('');
            });
        }
```

12. Close the post method by providing the data type that you expect the PHP function to return:

```
        }, 'html');
    });
```

LOGGING IN THE USER

The last step you need to do in the validation procedures is to give users a way to log in to their account.

The jQuery for the login function is nearly a duplicate of the registration, so I'll present it in its entirety:

```
$('#loginForm').submit(function(e){
    e.preventDefault();
    var formData = $(this).serialize();
    $.post('inc/peRegister.php', formData, function(data) {
        var returnValue = data;
        if(1 == returnValue){
            $('#loginWindow, #modalShade').fadeOut(function() {
                $('#loginForm input[name*="pe"]').val('');
                window.location = "4-2.php";
            });
```

```
        } else {
            $('body').append('<div id="li" class="errorModal">
         →  <h3>There is an error with your login</h3><p>Please
         →  try again...</div>');
            var modalMarginTop = ($('#li').height() + 60) / 2;
            var modalMarginLeft = ($('#li').width() + 60) / 2;
            $('#li').css({
                'margin-top' : -modalMarginTop,
                'margin-left' : -modalMarginLeft
            });
            $('#li').fadeIn().prepend('<a href="#"
             →  class="close_error"><img src="grfx/close_button.png"
             →  class="close_button" title="Close Window"
             →  alt="Close" /></a>');
            $('a.close_error').live('click', function() {
                $('#li').fadeOut(function() {
                    $('a.close_error, #li').remove();
                });
            });
        }
    }, 'html');
});
```

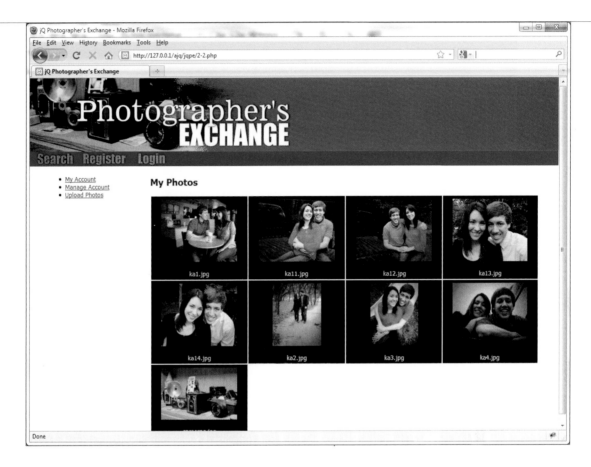

If the login is successful, the browser loads *chap4/4-2.php* (**Figure 4.5**), the user's account page.

Now that you are comfortable with basic jQuery AJAX, let's move on to using the jQuery AJAX functions to update content in the browser.

FIGURE 4.5 The user's account page is displayed on a successful login.

USING AJAX TO UPDATE CONTENT

In many cases, you'll want to use various jQuery AJAX functions to update visible Web-site content. Some content updates may be based on the user information for the current user, other updates may be based on requests performed by any user, such as information based on a search performed by the Web-site visitor.

Let's look at some techniques for using jQuery's AJAX methods to update content.

GETTING CONTENT BASED ON THE CURRENT USER

If you have been developing Web sites even for the shortest period of time, you are likely aware of query strings in the URL. Unless Web-site developers are using methods to hide the strings, you may have seen something similar to this:

```
http://www.website.com/?user=me&date=today
```

Everything past the question mark is a query string that can be used in a GET request to the server. Each item is set up in a *name=value* pair, which can be easily parsed by scripting languages like jQuery and PHP.

NOTE: Most forms utilize the POST method to request data from the server, but URLs are limited to the GET method. Most Web developers follow the rule of using GET when only retrieving data and using POST when sending data to the server that will invoke a change on the server.

GET requests are not limited to the URL. You can use GET as a form method or in AJAX. jQuery provides a shorthand method call for making this kind of request to the server, and conveniently, it is called get.

1. Open *chap4/4-2.php* to set up a get function to retrieve the current user's pictures into the Web browser. Rather than storing the jQuery code in a different file and including it, let's use a slightly different technique that is very valuable when small jQuery scripts are used.

2. Locate the closing </body> tag. Just before that tag, the jQuery AJAX get method will be set up to retrieve the user's pictures. Begin by inserting the script tag:

```
<script type="text/javascript">
```

3. Open the function by making sure that the document (the current Web page DOM information) is completely loaded:

```
$(document).ready(function() {
```

4. The first critical step in making sure that you get the right information from the database is to assign the value of the cookie set during login to a variable that can be used by jQuery. The information in the cookie is the user's name:

```
var cookieUser = '<?php echo $_COOKIE['photoex'];?>';
```

5. As stated earlier, the get method relies on *name=value* pairs to do its work properly. Make sure that the get request sends the cookie data to the server as a *name=value* pair:

```
$.get('inc/userPhoto.php', {photoUser: cookieUser},
→  function(data){
```

6. Load the information returned into the div with an id of myPhotos:

```
$('#myPhotos').html(data);
```

7. Close the get function with the data type that is expected to be returned from the PHP script. Once closed, set the closing </script> tag (the </body> tag is shown only for reference):

```
}, 'html');
    });
</script>
</body>
```

8. Before you can get the photos from the database, you need to create the photo table. So, run the *pephoto.sql* file located in the *chap4/sql* folder of the code download. The SQL file will also insert default data for the photos located in the *chap4/photos* folder.

In the PHP file *chap4/inc/userPhoto.php*, the SQL query uses the information contained in the photoUser variable:

```
$getImg = "SELECT `imgName`,`imgThumb` ";
$getImg .= "FROM `photoex`.`pephoto` ";
$getImg .= "WHERE `username` = '".$_GET['photoUser']."' ";
```

FIGURE 4.6 The user's photographs in tabular form.

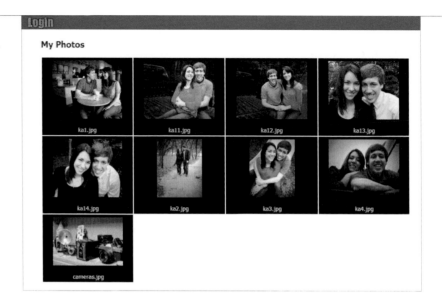

The user's photographs are retrieved and placed into a table for viewing. The results are illustrated in **Figure 4.6**.

Combining user data with the get method is very effective for pages where data unique to the user must be displayed. What about content that is not unique to the user? The get method has a cool little brother called load.

LOADING CONTENT BASED ON REQUEST

Of the jQuery AJAX shorthand methods, load is the simplest and easiest method for retrieving information from the server. It is especially useful if you want to call on new information that does not need data passed to it like you would do with the get or post methods. The syntax for load is short and sweet as well:

```
$('a[href="writeNew"]').click(function(e){
    e.preventDefault();
    $('#newArticle').load('inc/userWrite.php');
});
```

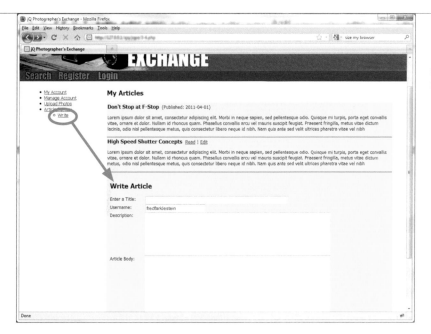

FIGURE 4.7 The form has been loaded into the page so that the user can write a new article.

Clicking on the Write link (**Figure 4.7**) invokes the load function, causing *chap4/inc/userWrite.php* to be loaded into the div with an id of newArticle.

There is one other really neat feature that load offers: You can use it to bring in just portions of other pages. For instance, to bring in a div with an id of part1 from another page, the syntax is as follows:

```
$('#newArticle').load('inc/anotherPage.html #part1');
```

Having the option of loading page portions can give you a great deal of design and organizational flexibility.

> **NOTE:** In Chapter 6, "Creating Application Interfaces," you'll use an example in which several widgets will be contained in one file that will be called by load as needed to complete the interface.

Not every Web site can use every AJAX feature that jQuery offers, so you'll leave the Photographer's Exchange Web site behind at this point. You'll develop stand-alone examples to demonstrate some of the other features and events available in jQuery's AJAX library.

LOADING SCRIPTS DYNAMICALLY

There are some cases in which you will need to load JavaScript or jQuery scripts just for one-time use in your Web pages and applications. jQuery provides a special AJAX shorthand method to do just that, getScript.

For this example, you'll use the code contained in *chap3/dvdCollection*, which is a small personal Web site designed to be used as a catalog of all the DVD and Blu-ray Discs that you own.

From time to time, you'll want to know just how many DVD and Blu-ray Discs you have, but it isn't really necessary to load the script that performs the counts and displays the result every time you use the site. jQuery's getScript method is the perfect remedy for loading scripts that you'll use infrequently.

1. Set up a script called *dvdcount.js* and place it in the *inc* directory of the DVD collection site. This is the script that getScript will load when called upon to do so.

2. Include the document ready functionality:

   ```
   $(document).ready(function(){
   ```

3. Each movie is contained in a div with a class of dvd. Assign the count of those div's to the variable totalCount:

   ```
   var totalCount = $('.dvd').length;
   ```

4. Use jQuery's :contains selector to help count the types of discs in the collection. The :contains selector is very handy for finding elements containing a specific string. Here it is used to find the text "DVD" or "Blu-ray" in the h3 element:

   ```
   var dvdCount = $('h3:contains("DVD")').length;
   var brCount = $('h3:contains("Blu-ray")').length;
   ```

5. Set up the modal window to show the user the information. This is the same technique used in Chapter 2 and Chapter 3, so I won't cover each step in detail:

   ```
   var movieModal = '<div class="movieModal">Total Movies:
     → '+totalCount+'<br />DVD: '+dvdCount+'<br />Blu-ray:
     → '+brCount+'</div>';
   ```

```
$('body').append(movieModal);
var modalMarginTop = ($('.movieModal').height() + 40) / 2;
var modalMarginLeft = ($('.movieModal').width() + 40) / 2;
$('.movieModal').css({
    'margin-top' : -modalMarginTop,
    'margin-left' : -modalMarginLeft
});
```

The modal will only pop up for a moment before fading out:

```
$('.movieModal').fadeIn('slow', function(){
    $(this).fadeOut(2500, function() {
        $(this).remove();
    });
});
});
```

The main page for the DVD catalog site is *chap4/dvdCollection/4-5.php*. Let's take a moment to set it up.

1. Enter the information for the header:

```
<!DOCTYPE html>
<html lang="en">
    <head>
        <meta charset="utf-8">
        <title>DVD Collection Catalog</title>
        <link rel="stylesheet" href="css/dvd.css"
        → type="text/css" />
```

2. Include the jQuery file so that all of the interactions will run properly:

```
<script type="text/javascript"
 → src="inc/jquery-1.5.min.js"></script>
</head>
```

3. Set up the body next:

```
<body>
<h2>DVD Collection Catalog</h2>
<div class="menuContainer">
```

4. Set up the menu section carefully, because you'll use these elements to call other scripts:

```
<ul class="menu">
    <li id="add">Add</li>
    <li id="summary">Summary</li>
</ul>
</div>
<br />
```

5. Set up the div that will house the content of the page:

```
<div class="content"></div>
```

6. Create the section containing the jQuery scripts you'll use to load information into the page along with the function that loads *chap4/dvdCollection/inc/getdvd.php*. The PHP is called by the jQuery load method to get the information about the DVD collection:

```
<script type="text/javascript">
    $(document).ready(function(){
        $('.content').load('inc/getdvd.php');
```

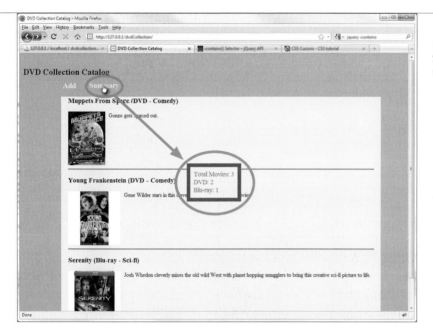

FIGURE 4.8 Clicking on the Summary element loads and runs the *dvdcount.js* script.

7. Bind the `click` method to the list item with an `id` of summary. This will call `getScript` to run the jQuery script created earlier, *dvdcount.js*:

```
$('#summary').click(function() {
$.getScript('inc/dvdcount.js');
});
});
</script>
```

8. Close out the HTML:

```
</body>
</html>
```

Clicking the Summary element on the Web page causes the *dvdcount.js* script to be loaded and run, showing the modal window complete with counts (**Figure 4.8**). The modal window then slowly fades away.

You will find many cases where loading and running scripts on the fly will enhance your Web sites and applications.

Next, you'll turn your attention to many of jQuery's AJAX extras and learn how to apply them practically.

USING JQUERY'S AJAX EXTRAS

In addition to the shorthand methods, jQuery provides many useful methods and helpers to give you ways to use AJAX efficiently. These methods range from low-level interfaces to global event handlers, all of which, when applied properly, will make your programs and Web sites more effective.

Let's look at these extras, starting with the low-level interfaces.

WORKING WITH LOW-LEVEL INTERFACES

jQuery's low-level AJAX interfaces provide the most detailed approach to AJAX functions. This kind of detail makes the low-level interfaces quite flexible but introduces additional complexity due to all of the options available.

One way to combat the complexity of having an extensive choice of options is to use a method to set up options that do not change frequently. Take a look at the simplest of the low-level interfaces, ajaxSetup:

```
$.ajaxSetup({
    url: ajaxProcessing.php,
    type: 'POST'
});
```

The ajaxSetup method allows you to provide options that will be used with every AJAX request. You can set all of the AJAX options available (over 25 of them!) using ajaxSetup. This is very convenient if you need to make repeated AJAX requests to the same URL or use the same password each time you make a request. In many cases, developers will put all of their server-side AJAX handlers in the same file on the server. Using ajaxSetup shortens their AJAX calls, including the shorthand methods. Given the current example of ajaxSetup, your post method could be configured like this:

```
$.post({ data: formData });
```

The only thing you need to supply to the post function is the data to be handled by *ajaxProcessing.php*. One advantage of using the ajaxSetup method is that you can override any of the ajaxSetup options in the individual AJAX calls that you make.

The low-level interface that you will see in use most is the straight ajax method. It is the function that is wrapped by the shorthand methods and is at the very heart of all of jQuery's AJAX calls. The ajax method is capable of accepting all of the options that can be used with jQuery's AJAX requests. Perhaps the best way to understand the low-level AJAX method is to compare it to one of the shorthand methods you used earlier. Here is the post method that you used to check to make sure the user name was available:

```
$.post('inc/peRegister.php', {
    formName: 'register',
    penewuser: newName
}, function(data){
    var usernameCount = data;
    if(1 == usernameCount){
        $('#penewuser').next('.error').css('display', 'inline');
    } else {
        $('#penewuser').next('.error').css('display', 'none');
    }
}, 'html');
```

Here is the same request using jQuery's low-level ajax method:

```
$.ajax({
    type: 'POST',
    url: 'inc/peRegister.php',
    data: 'formName=register&penewuser='+newName+'',
    success: function(data){
        var usernameCount = data;
        if(1 == usernameCount){
```

```
            $('#penewuser').next('.error').css('display', 'inline');
        } else {
            $('#penewuser').next('.error').css('display', 'none');
        }
    },
    dataType: 'html'
});
```

The differences are fairly obvious, such as declaring the method that AJAX should use to convey the information to the server (type: 'POST'), specifying the way that raw data is formatted (data: 'formName=register&penewuser='+newName+'',) and ensuring that the success method is implicitly defined (success: function(data){…}).

Take a tour of jQuery's ajax API at http://api.jquery.com/jQuery.ajax to see all of the options available for use with this method.

Now that you can send information to the server and receive information back from your server-side processes, you need to make sure that your users are informed that an AJAX action is taking place. jQuery provides several helper functions that make it easy for you to do just that.

TRIGGERING EVENTS BEFORE AND AFTER THE AJAX CALL

In many cases, your jQuery AJAX functions will happen so quickly that users may not even know that their actions achieved the desired result. In other cases, the AJAX process may be lengthy and require that users wait for results. jQuery provides four methods that you can use to keep users informed: ajaxStart, ajaxSend, ajaxComplete, and ajaxStop.

It is important to understand that there is an order to these four functions. You can call any number of AJAX processes during any given event. For this reason, you may want to know not only when the first AJAX function starts, but also when each subsequent AJAX method gets called and completes. Then you may want to register that all of the AJAX calls have completed. If you imagine jQuery AJAX events as a stack of items as in **Figure 4.9**, you'll see how the jQuery AJAX engine defines the order of the events and their calls.

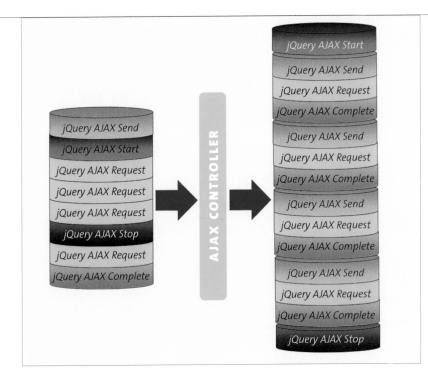

FIGURE 4.9 The initial jQuery events are stacked up by the developer and then ordered and processed by jQuery's AJAX engine.

Let's take a close look at how to use the ajaxStart and ajaxStop methods by giving users a visual queue during a data- and file-submission event in the DVD Collection Catalog.

1. Open *chap4/4-6.php*.

   In *4-6.php* you will see a form (**Figure 4.10** on the next page) that accepts user input and provides a method for uploading a file. This combination is not unusual, but it will require that you pay careful attention when writing the PHP and jQuery to handle the data transfer and file upload.

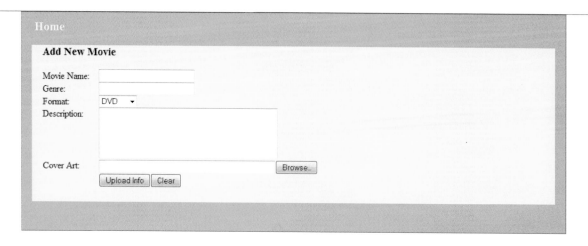

FIGURE 4.10 The form that users will fill out to add movies to their personal database.

Two PHP scripts will handle the data supplied in the form: one for the movie cover art upload (not really AJAX, remember?) and one for the data input into the form.

2. Create a file called *chap4/dvdCollection/inc/**dvdcover.php*** to set up the image upload first.

3. Set up the path for the cover art:

   ```
   $coverPath = "../cover_art/";
   ```

4. Make sure that the file is submitted properly and has no errors:

   ```
   if ($_FILES["movieCover"]["error"] == UPLOAD_ERR_OK) {
   ```

5. Set up the variables to hold the information about the uploaded file (this is the same technique that you used for file uploads in Chapter 3):

   ```
   $tmpName = $_FILES["movieCover"]["tmp_name"];
   $coverName = $_FILES["movieCover"]["name"];
   ```

6. Create the regular expression used to check the file extension of the uploaded file:

   ```
   $regexFileExt = "/\.(jpg|jpeg|png)$/i";
   ```

7. Test the file extension to see if it matches one allowed by the regular expression:

```
if(preg_match($regexFileExt, $coverName)){
```

8. Check the file again by making sure it really is the right kind of file according to its first few bytes:

```
$arrEXIFType = array(IMAGETYPE_JPEG, IMAGETYPE_PNG);
if(in_array(exif_imagetype($tmpName), $arrEXIFType)){
```

9. Set up the file's new name and path, and place them into the variable $newCover:

```
$newCover = $coverPath.$coverName;
```

10. Move the properly named file to its permanent directory:

```
move_uploaded_file($tmpName, $newCover);

        }

    }

}
```

Now that you've completed the PHP script for the file upload, you can create the PHP script that will be called by the jQuery AJAX post method to update the database.

1. Create a file called **postdvd.php** and store it in the *chap4/dvdCollection/inc* folder.

   Only two actions are contained in *postdvd.php*: one to connect to the database and one to run the query that will perform the database update.

2. Set up the database connection first (be sure to use the user name and password that you have set up for your database):

```
if(!$dbc = mysql_connect('localhost', 'username', 'password')){
    echo mysql_error() . "\n";
    exit();
}
```

3. Introduce a little sleep timer to slow down the process. This will allow the animated loading graphic to be displayed by ajaxStart in the jQuery function that will be created (typically, the database operation is very fast—so fast that the user may not realize that something has occurred.):

```
sleep(2);
```

4. Create the SQL query that will accept the values from the AJAX post method to update the database with:

```
$insertMovie = "INSERT INTO `dvdcollection`.`dvd` ";
$insertMovie .= "(`name`,`genre`,`format`,`description`,
  → `cover`) ";
$insertMovie .= "VALUES(";
$insertMovie .= "'".$_POST['movieName']."',";
$insertMovie .= "'".$_POST['movieGenre']."',";
$insertMovie .= "'".$_POST['movieFormat']."',";
$insertMovie .= "'".$_POST['movieDescription']."',";
$insertMovie .= "'cover_art/".$_POST['movieCover']."' ";
$insertMovie .= ")";
```

NOTE: Make sure that you run the SQL chap4/dvdCollection/sql/create_collection_table.sql script in your database platform to set up and populate the table for the DVD collection.

5. Call the mysql_query function to run the SQL query:

```
if(!($movieInfo = mysql_query($insertMovie, $dbc))){
    echo mysql_error();
    echo mysql_errno();
    exit();
}
```

With the PHP scripts complete, you can now turn your attention to the jQuery functions. All of the jQuery functions will be placed into the file *inc/movieUp.js*.

1. Start the file by defining the ajaxStart method:

```
$('body').ajaxStart(function(){
```

The ajaxStart function will be called as soon as an AJAX request is made. The method can be bound to any element available in the DOM and is bound to the body element for use here. You can define any processes that you want within the ajaxStart method.

2. For this file and data upload, create a modal pop-up window to give the users a visual clue that something is occurring:

```
var waitingModal = '<div class="waitingModal">
→ <img src="grfx/loading.gif" border="0" /></div>';
$('body').append(waitingModal);
var modalMarginTop = ($('.waitingModal').height() + 40) / 2;
var modalMarginLeft = ($('.waitingModal').width() + 40) / 2;
$('.waitingModal').css({
    'margin-top' : -modalMarginTop,
    'margin-left' : -modalMarginLeft
});
$('.waitingModal').fadeIn('slow');
});
```

The technique used to create the modal window is no different than what you have used previously in the book.

3. Bind the ajaxStop method to the body element (remember that methods like ajaxStart and ajaxStop can be bound to any element). When the AJAX request is complete, you'll want to clear the form and remove the modal from view so that the user knows the process is finished:

```
$('body').ajaxStop(function(){
```

4. Clear the form elements so that the user can use the form to add another movie. Just like using ajaxStart, you can define any process within the ajaxStop function:

```
$('#addMovie input[name*="movie"]').val('');

$('#addMovie textarea').val('');
```

Be very specific with your jQuery selectors when choosing which form elements to clear. For example, using just $('#addMovie input') will also clear the form's buttons, and that would confuse the user.

5. Fade away the modal indicator and remove it from the DOM. This is the last part of the process defined in the ajaxStop method:

```
$('.waitingModal').fadeOut('slow', function(){
    $(this).remove();
});
});
```

6. Begin the form handler by binding the form addMovie to the submit method:

```
$('#addMovie').submit(function(){
```

7. Upload the image using the iframe method that was defined in Chapter 3:

```
var iframeName = ('iframeUpload');
var iframeTemp = $('<iframe name="'+iframeName+'"
 → src="about:blank" />');
iframeTemp.css('display', 'none');
$('body').append(iframeTemp);
$(this).attr({
    action: 'inc/dvdcover.php',
    method: 'post',
    enctype: 'multipart/form-data',
    encoding: 'multipart/form-data',
    target: iframeName
});
```

8. Once the image upload is complete, remove the `iframe` from the DOM:

```
setTimeout(function(){
    iframeTemp.remove();
}, 1000);
```

FIGURE 4.11 The ajaxStart method has called the waiting indicator.

9. Prepare the data to be used in the post method. Because information in a textarea cannot be serialized with normal jQuery methods, create a text string that sets up the textarea value as if it were serialized by making the information a *name=value* pair:

```
var coverData = '&movieCover=' +
→  $('input[name="movieCover"]').val();
```

10. Serialize the remainder of the form data:

```
var formData = $(this).serialize();
```

11. Once the form data has been processed by the `serialize` function, concatenate the two strings together in the `uploadData` variable:

```
var uploadData = formData + coverData;
```

12. Call the jQuery AJAX shorthand method post to upload the data:

```
$.post('inc/postdvd.php', uploadData);
});
```

When the movie data form is submitted, the jQuery AJAX engine will see that there is a post occurring during the process, triggering the `ajaxStart` method. **Figure 4.11** shows the modal loading indicator called by `ajaxStart`.

Once the post process has completed, the `ajaxStop` method is triggered, causing the modal waiting indicator to fade out.

Now that you have learned to handle AJAX calls and the data they return, you need to learn how to handle one of the Web's fastest-growing data types, JSON.

TIP: If you need animated graphics to indicate to your users that something is occurring in the background, check out www.ajaxload.info. There you can generate several different animated graphics in a wide array of colors.

USING JSON

JSON (JavaScript Object Notation) has become a popular and lightweight way to transmit data packages for various uses over the Internet. In many ways, JSON is more popular than XML for delivering data quickly and efficiently. JSON data can be easily used with the jQuery AJAX shorthand method especially designed to handle the JSON data type, getJSON.

So what exactly is JSON?

To understand JSON, you need a little lesson in JavaScript's object literal notation. *Object literal notation* is an explicit way of creating an object and is the most robust way of setting up a JavaScript object. Here is an example:

```
var person = {
    name: "Jay",
    occupation: "developer",
    stats: ["blonde", "blue", "fair"],
    walk: function (){alert(this.name+ 'is walking');}
};
```

The person object has been literally defined as name: value pairs, including a nested array (stats) and a method to make the object walk. It is a very tidy way to describe an object.

The following commands interact with the person object:

```
person.walk(); //alerts 'Jay is walking'
alert(person.stats[1]); // alerts 'blue'
```

JSON is a subset of the object literal notation, essentially the *name: value* pairs that describe an object. A JSON array can contain multiple objects. The key to being successful with JSON is making sure that it is well-formed. JSON must have matching numbers of opening and closing brackets and curly braces (the braces must be in the correct order); the names and values in the *name : value* pairs must be quoted properly; and commas must separate each *name: value* pair.

To illustrate this, look at the JSON for the person object:

```
var myJSONobject = {"person":[{
    "name":"Jay",
    "occupation":"developer",
    "stats":[{
        "hair":"blonde",
        "eyes":"blue",
        "skin":"fair"
    }]
  }]
};
```

It's important to note that the JSON object does not contain any methods or functions that can be executed. JSON specifically excludes these from the notation because JSON is only meant to be a vehicle for transmitting data.

SETTING UP A JSON REQUEST

Twitter has undoubtedly become one of the most popular social media outlets since the dawn of the Internet. Twitter has made an API available for those who want to extend the use of Twitter to their own Web pages and applications. One of the most popular uses of the Twitter API is to include recent tweets in personal Web sites and blogs.

Taking advantage of the API can be as simple or as complex as you want it to be. Let's build a simple widget to obtain your last ten tweets for inclusion in a Web page.

The tweet data is returned from Twitter in the JSONP format. JSONP is known as "JSON with Padding." Under normal circumstances, you cannot make AJAX requests outside of the domain the request originates from (**Figure 4.12** on the next page). JSONP relies on a JavaScript quirk: `<script>` elements are allowed to make those cross-domain requests.

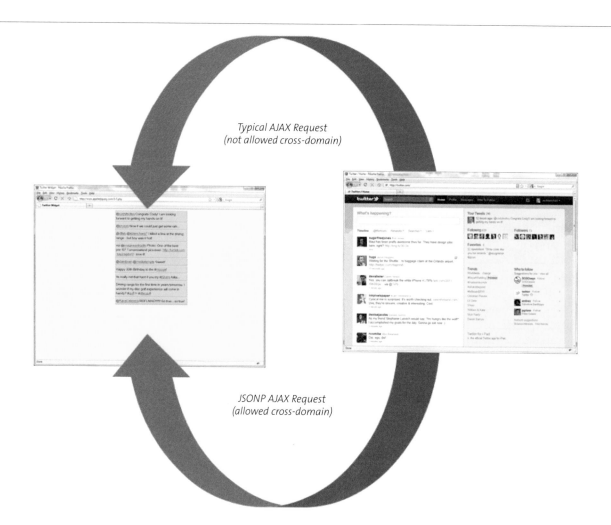

*Typical AJAX Request
(not allowed cross-domain)*

*JSONP AJAX Request
(allowed cross-domain)*

FIGURE 4.12 The only way you can make a cross-domain request is with JSONP.

To make this work, the JSON must be returned in a function. Using the JSON object created earlier, the JSONP would look like this:

```
myJSONfunction({"person":[{"name":"Jay", "occupation":"developer",
    "stats":[{"hair":"blonde","eyes":"blue","skin":"fair"}]}]});
```

If it looks like gibberish to you now, don't worry; as you walk through the function being built to get JSON data from Twitter, it will become much clearer. Let's build the entire file, including CSS, from scratch.

1. Create a file called **4-7.php** in the *chap4* folder.

2. Set up the DOCTYPE and include the basic head, title, and character set declarations:

```
<!DOCTYPE html>

<html>

    <head>

    <meta http-equiv="Content-Type" content="text/html;
 →  charset=utf-8" />

    <title>Twitter Widget</title>
```

3. Provide a reference to the jQuery source that you will be using. Make sure that the path is correct; in this case the path is *inc/jquery-1.5.2.min.js*:

```
<script type="text/javascript"
 →  src="inc/jquery-1.5.min.js"></script>
```

4. Create the style information for the Twitter widget:

```
<style type="text/css">
    body {
        background-color: #FFFFCC;
    }
    #tw {
        position: relative;
        width: 350px;
        left: 50%;
        margin-left: -175px;
    }
    .tweet {
        font-family: "Lucida Grande","Arial Unicode MS",
 →      sans-serif;
        width: 350px;
```

```
        background-color: #99FFCC;

        padding: 5px;

        border-right: 2px solid #66CC99;

        border-bottom: 3px solid #66CC99;

        margin-bottom: 2px;

    }

</style>
```

5. Close out the head section of the page:

```
</head>
```

The body section for the widget is very simple: Add a div with an id of tw to which the tweets will be appended:

```
<body>

    <div id="tw"></div>
```

The jQuery script to get the tweets is very short but requires that you pay attention to detail. You will make the names and hash tags clickable so that they have the same functionality they have on the Twitter Web site. Any links included in a tweet will also be clickable, opening a new browser window to show the information.

1. Start the jQuery function by opening a script tag and inserting the document-ready function:

```
<script type="text/javascript">

$(document).ready(function() {
```

2. Create the URL to access Twitter and store the URL in the variable twitterURL:

```
var twitterURL ='http://twitter.com/statuses/
  user_timeline.json?screen_name=
  YOUR_TWITTER_USER_NAME&count=10&callback=?';
```

Be sure to replace YOUR_TWITTER_USER_NAME with your actual Twitter user name. It is very important to make sure that the URL is formatted with the query string (*name=value* pairs) that will be used by getJSON during the request. Send three options to Twitter: your Twitter screen_name, the count of the number of tweets to return, and most important, the callback. It is the callback option that lets Twitter know that you expect the return data to be JSONP.

3. Once the URL is formed, open the getJSON request method by sending the URL and defining the getJSON callback option:

```
$.getJSON(twitterURL, function(data){
```

> **NOTE:** The callback option for the query string is not the same as the callback for the *getJSON* request.

4. The JSONP has been returned from Twitter at this point. Set up a loop through the data contained in the function. Treat the data as members of an array called item:

```
$.each(data, function(i, item){
```

5. Contain the tweet in a *name: value* pair with the *name* of text. Assign this item to the variable tweetText:

```
var tweetText = item.text;
```

6. Use regular expressions to locate URLs, @ tags, and hash(#) tags in the tweet so that you can give each the proper treatment. Look for URL's first:

```
tweetText = tweetText.replace
→ (/http:\/\/\S+/g, '<a href="$&"
→ target="_blank">$&</a>');
```

The regular expression /http:\/\/\S+/g matches text beginning with http:// and ending in a space, which would typically indicate a URL. The /g (global) says to match all URLs in the string contained in tweetText. The URLs are turned into links by replacing the URL with an anchor tag containing the URL as both the href and the text of the link. In JavaScript the $& property contains the last item matched by a regular expression. Because the URL was the last item matched, it can be replaced into an anchor tag by using the $& property.

7. Twitter prefixes user names with the @ symbol. So, search `tweetText` for words beginning with the @ symbol:

```
tweetText = tweetText.replace(/(@)(\w+)/g,
→ ' $1<a href="http://twitter.com/$2"
→ target="_blank">$2</a>');
```

Here, the regular expression `/(@)(\w+)/g` indicates that all words beginning with the @ symbol are replaced by the appropriate anchor tag to open a browser window for users' tweets. The $1 and $2 contain the information matched in each parenthesis, which is used to include those matches in the replacement text.

8. Turn your attention to the hash tags now and use a technique similar to the one you used for replacing the @ symbol:

```
tweetText = tweetText.replace(/(#)(\w+)/g,
→ ' $1<a href="http://search.twitter.com/
→ search?q=%23$2" target="_blank">$2
→ </a>');
```

9. Once the `tweetText` has been completely manipulated to insert all of the anchor tags, place it into a div. Then append the new div to the existing div (id="tw") that was set up as part of the original content for the page:

```
$("#tw").append('<div class="tweet">
→ '+tweetText+'</div>');
```

10. Close out the jQuery function and HTML tags for the page:

```
            });
          });
        });
      </script>
    </body>
  </html>
```

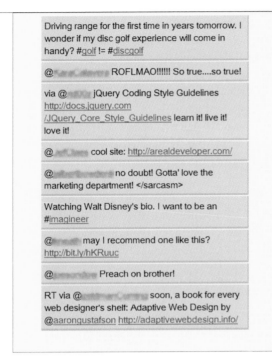

Driving range for the first time in years tomorrow. I wonder if my disc golf experience will come in handy? #golf != #discgolf

@█████████ ROFLMAO!!!!!! So true....so true!

via @█████ jQuery Coding Style Guidelines http://docs.jquery.com /JQuery_Core_Style_Guidelines learn it! live it! love it!

@████ cool site: http://arealdeveloper.com/

@████████ no doubt! Gotta' love the marketing department! </sarcasm>

Watching Walt Disney's bio. I want to be an #imagineer

@██████ may I recommend one like this? http://bit.ly/hKRuuc

@█████ Preach on brother!

RT via @████████████ soon, a book for every web designer's shelf: Adaptive Web Design by @aarongustafson http://adaptivewebdesign.info/

FIGURE 4.13 The Twitter widget retrieves the last few posts that you made.

11. Upload the page to a server, and load the page into a browser. You should achieve the results that you see in **Figure 4.13**.

With all of the data traveling back and forth between clients and servers, including servers not under your control, it is only natural to be concerned about the security of the information that you and your Web-site visitors send in AJAX requests. Let's address those concerns next.

SECURING **AJAX REQUESTS**

One of the vexing problems with Web sites and applications is that users will either inadvertently or purposely submit data through your Web site that can cause harm to your databases and servers. It is important that you take as many steps as possible to guard against the input and transmission of bad or malformed data.

Several of these steps have been covered already, including using regular expressions to guide the user to input the right kind of data and making sure that cookies are set uniquely for each Web visitor. As an older, and much wiser, mentor said to me, "Locking the gate in this way only keeps the honest people from climbing the fence."

Even with regular expressions in place for form fields, you cannot stop the transmission of the data because the form can still be submitted. So, what are some of the measures you can take to prevent users from submitting potentially harmful data?

- Prevent form submission by "graying" out the Submit button on forms until all of the regular expression rules for each form field have been met.

- Use cookies to uniquely identify the user (more precisely, the user's computer) based on registration information and check cookie data against a database during transmission of user-supplied data.

- Clean user-supplied data when it arrives at the back-end process to make sure the data doesn't contain harmful statements or characters.

- Transmit the data over a secure connection (HTTPS [HyperText Transfer Protocol Secure]) to prevent outsiders from "sniffing" information traveling from and to the Web browser.

NOTE: For more information on HTTPS, visit the Electronic Frontier Foundation's Web site at www.eff.org/https-everywhere.

These techniques should be used in conjunction with each other to present the safest experience for the user and the Web-site owner. Let's walk through some of these techniques.

PREVENTING FORM SUBMISSION

Let's return to the Photographer's Exchange Web site and make some changes to the HTML file containing the registration form as well as the jQuery script that supports the form.

1. Open *chap4/4-2.php* and locate the section of the script where jQuery scripts are included. You'll find these include declarations between the head tags.

2. Change the following highlighted line to point to the updated *jqpe.js* file:

```
<script type="text/javascript"
→ src="inc/jquery-1.5.min.js"></script>

<script type="text/javascript"
→ src="inc/jquery.ez-bg-resize.js"></script>

<script type="text/javascript"
→ src="inc/spritenav.js"></script>

<script type="text/javascript"
→ src="inc/carousel.js"></script>

<script type="text/javascript"
→ src="inc/jqpe.js"></script>

<script type="text/javascript"
→ src="inc/peAjax.js"></script>
```

    After the change, the line will look like this:

```
<script type="text/javascript"
→ src="inc/jqpeUpdated.js"></script>
```

3. Save the file as ***chap4/4-8.php***.

4. Open *chap4/inc/jqpe.js* and save it as ***chap4/inc/jqpeUpdated.js***. Add the code for the error count function. Start by initializing the $submitErrors variable:

```
var submitErrors = 0;
```

5. Declare a function called errorCount:

```
function errorCount(errors) {
```

6. Set the argument variable errors to be equal to the submitErrors variable:

```
errors = submitErrors;
```

7. If the error count is zero, you want to enable the submit button. So, remove the disabled attribute from the button. Use the jQuery attribute selectors to select the proper button:

```
if(0 == errors){
    $('input[type="submit"][value="Register"]').
    →  removeAttr('disabled');
```

8. If the error count is not zero, the submit button will be disabled. Use the same selector syntax and add the disabled attribute to the button:

```
} else {
    $('input[type="submit"][value="Register"]').
    →  attr('disabled','disabled');
}
```

9. Close out the function :

```
}
```

Once the function is in place, you'll need to make some changes to the password and email validation functions that were created previously.

1. In *jqpeUpdated.js* locate the password validation function that begins with the comment /*make sure password is not blank */. Insert the two new lines of code highlighted here:

```
/* make sure that password is not blank */
    $(function() {
        var passwordLength = $('#penewpass').val().length;
        if(passwordLength == 0){
            $('#penewpass').next('.error').css('display',
            →  'inline');
            errorCount(submitErrors++);
            $('#penewpass').change(function() {
```

```
                    $(this).next('.error').css('display', 'none');
                    errorCount(submitErrors--);
            });
        }
    });
```

If the password is blank (having a length of zero), the errorCount function is called and the submitErrors variable is incremented by a count of one.

```
errorCount(submitErrors++);
```

After a password has been entered, the error is cleared and the error count can be reduced by decrementing submitErrors:

```
errorCount(submitErrors--);
```

2. Locate the email validation function. It begins with the comment /* validate e-mail address in register form */. Add the same calls to the errorCount function where indicated by the following highlights:

```
/* validate e-mail address in register form */
    $(function(){
        var emailLength = $('#email').val().length;
        if(emailLength == 0){
            $('#email').next('.error').css('display',
        →  'inline');
            errorCount(submitErrors++);
            $('#email').change(function() {
            var regexEmail = /^[a-zA-Z0-9._-]+@[a-zA-Z0-9.-]+
        →  \.[a-zA-Z]{2,4}$/;
            var inputEmail = $(this).val();
            var resultEmail = regexEmail.test(inputEmail);
            if(resultEmail){
                $(this).next('.error').css('display', 'none');
                errorCount(submitErrors--);
```

FIGURE 4.14 The Register
button is grayed out. It is not
available to the user until all
errors are cleared.

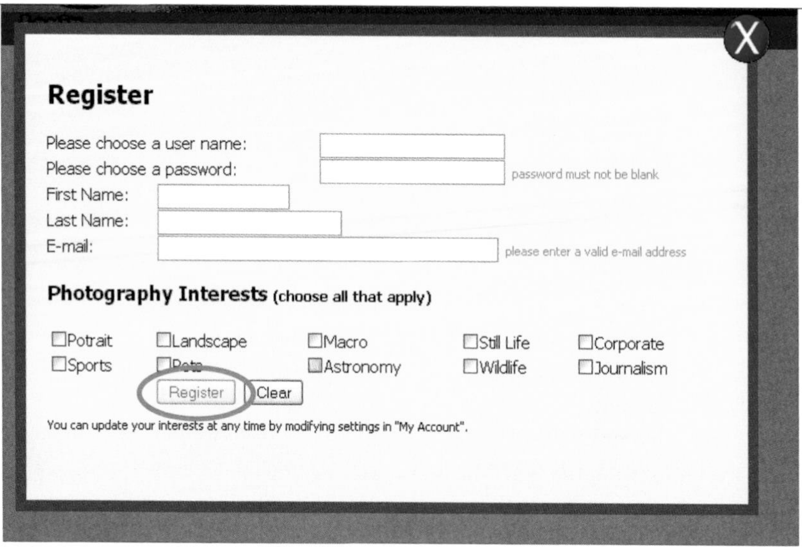

Register

Please choose a user name:

Please choose a password: password must not be blank

First Name:

Last Name:

E-mail: please enter a valid e-mail address

Photography Interests (choose all that apply)

☐Potrait   ☐Landscape   ☐Macro   ☐Still Life   ☐Corporate
☐Sports   ☐Pets   ☐Astronomy   ☐Wildlife   ☐Journalism

[Register] [Clear]

You can update your interests at any time by modifying settings in "My Account".

```
                    }
                });
            }
        });
```

When the page first loads, submitErrors gets incremented twice—once by each of the validation functions. The total error count prior to the form being filled out is two. Because the submitErrors has a value of two, the submit button is disabled, as illustrated in **Figure 4.14**.

As each function is cleared of its error, the submitErrors variable is decremented until it finally attains a value of zero. When the value of submitErrors is zero, the errorCount function removes the disabled attribute from the submit button and the form can be submitted normally.

This technique can be applied to any number of form fields that you need to validate, but it really isn't enough to prevent malicious users from trying to hack your site. Let's take a look at another technique you can add to your Web-site application model, giving each user cookies.

USING COOKIES TO IDENTIFY USERS

Giving users cookies sounds very pleasant. But it really means that you want to identify users to make sure they are allowed to use the forms and data on your Web site. What you don't want to do is put sensitive information into cookies. Cookies can be stolen, read, and used.

Personally, I'm not a big fan of "remember me cookies" because the longer it takes a cookie to expire, the longer the potentially malicious user has to grab and use information in the cookie. I'd rather cookies expire when the user closes the browser. This would reduce the chance that someone could log in to the user's computer and visit the same sites to gain information or copy the cookies to another location.

What should you store in the cookie? One technique that you can employ that is very effective is storing a unique token in the cookie that can be matched to the user during the user's current session. Let's modify the Photographer's Exchange login process to store a token in the user's database record. The token will be changed each time the user logs in to the site, and you will use the token to retrieve other data about the user as needed.

1. Open *chap4/inc/peRegister.php* and locate the section that starts with the comment /* if the login is good */. You will insert new code to create and save the token into the newly created database column.

2. The first line that you need to add creates a unique value to tokenize. Concatenate the user name contained in $_POST['pename'] with a time stamp from PHP's time function. PHP's time function returns the time in seconds since January 1, 1970. Store that in the variable $tokenValue, as shown in the following highlighted line:

```
/* if the login is good */
if(1 == $loginCount){
    if(isset($_POST['remember'])){
    $tokenValue = $_POST['pename'].time("now");
```

3. Modify the information to be stored in $peCookieValue by hashing the $tokenValue with an MD5 (Message Digest Algorithm) hash:

```
$peCookieValue = hash('md5', $tokenValue);
$peCookieExpire = time()+(60*60*24*365);
```

```
        $domain = ($_SERVER['HTTP_HOST'] != 'localhost') ?
    →   $_SERVER['HTTP_HOST'] : false;

        setcookie('photoex', $peCookieValue, $peCookieExpire, '/',
    →   $domain, false);

        echo $loginCount;

    } else {
```

The MD5 hash algorithm is a cryptographic hash that takes a string and converts it to a 32-bit hexadecimal number. The hexadecimal number is typically very unique and is made more so here by the use of the time function combined with the user's name.

4. Make the same modifications in the section of the code where no "remember me" value is set:

```
        $tokenValue = $_POST['pename'].time("now");

        $peCookieValue = hash('md5', $tokenValue);

        $peCookieExpire = 0;

        $domain = ($_SERVER['HTTP_HOST'] != 'localhost') ?
    →   $_SERVER['HTTP_HOST'] : false;

        setcookie('photoex', $peCookieValue, $peCookieExpire, '/',
    →   $domain, false);

        echo $loginCount;
```

5. Add the code that will update the database with the new value:

```
        $updateUser = "UPDATE `photoex`.`peuser` ";

        $updateUser .= "SET `token` = '".$peCookieValue."' ";

        $updateUser .= "WHERE `username` = '".$_POST['pename']."' ";

        if(!($updateData = mysql_query($updateUser, $dbc))){
            echo mysql_errno();
            exit();
        }
```

6. Open *chap4/4-8.php* and log in to the site with a known good user name and password. The cookie will be set with the token, and the token information will be set in the database. You can use your browser's built-in cookie viewer (for **Figure 4.15**, I used Tools > Page Info > Security > View Cookies in the Firefox browser) to examine the value stored in the cookie.

Using the value of the token, you can retrieve needed information about the user so that the data can be entered into forms or the appropriate photographs can be displayed. Next, let's take a look at cleaning up user-supplied data.

CLEANSING USER-SUPPLIED DATA

One additional step that you can take to make sure that user-supplied data is safe once it reaches the server is to use your client-side scripting language to ensure that the data is handled safely and securely.

A less than savory visitor may visit your site and copy your visible Web pages and functions. Once copied, modifications can be made to your jQuery scripts to remove some of the controls (regular expressions for instance) that you have placed around data. Your first line of defense against that is to replicate those controls in your server-side scripts.

1. Using email validations as an example, open *peRegister.php* (*chap4/inc/ peRegister.php*) to modify it.

2. Locate the section of the code that begins with the comment `/* if the registration form has a valid username & password insert the data */` and supply this regular expression:

```
$regexEmail = '/^[a-zA-Z0-9._-]+@[a-zA-Z0-9.-]+\.[a-zA-Z]{2,4}$/';
```

This is the same regular expression used in the jQuery function to validate email addresses into the registration form.

3. Test the value posted against the regular expression with PHP's `preg_match` function:

```
preg_match($regexEmail, $_POST['email'], $match);
```

4. The test result, a 1 if there is a match or a 0 if there isn't a match, is placed into the variable $match that is declared in the `preg_match` function. Use this result to modify the `$_POST['email']` variable:

```
if(1 == $match){
    $_POST['email'] = $_POST['email'];
} else {
    $_POST['email'] = 'E-MAIL ADDRESS NOT VALID';
}
```

The data from the `$_POST['email']` variable is used in the SQL query that inserts the data into the database.

Many languages, such as PHP, include specific functions for data cleansing. Let's take a look at two PHP functions that you can use to clean up data before it is entered into a database: `htmlspecialchars()` and `mysql_real_escape_string()`.

Cleaning up information submitted in HTML format is a simple matter of wrapping the data in PHP's `htmlspecialchars` function. Given a form like this:

```
<form name="search" action="inc/search.php" method="post">
    <label class="label" for="pesearch">Search For: </label>
    <input type="text" name="pesearch" id="pesearch" size="64" /><br />
    <label class="label"> </label>
    <input type="submit" value="Search" />
```

```
<input type="reset" value="Clear" />
</form>
```

The PHP htmlspecialchars function replaces certain characters and returns:

```
&lt;form name=&quot;search&quot; action=&quot;inc/search.php&quot;
⟶  method=&quot;post&quot;&gt;&lt;label class=&quot;label&quot;
⟶  for=&quot;pesearch&quot;&gt;Search For: &lt;/label&gt;&lt;input
⟶  type=&quot;text&quot; name=&quot;pesearch&quot;
⟶  id=&quot;pesearch&quot; size=&quot;64&quot; /&gt;&lt;br
⟶  /&gt;&lt;label class=&quot;label&quot;&gt; &lt;
⟶  /label&gt;&lt;input type=&quot;submit&quot;
⟶  value=&quot;Search&quot; /&gt;&lt;input type=&quot;reset&quot;
⟶  value=&quot;Clear&quot; /&gt;&lt;/form&gt;
```

The following characters have been changed:

- Ampersand (&) becomes '&'

- Double quote (") becomes '"'

- Single quote (') becomes '''

- The less than bracket (<) becomes '<'

- The greater than bracket (>) becomes '>'

Using PHP's htmlspecialchars function makes user-supplied HTML data much safer to use in your Web sites and databases. PHP does provide a function to reverse the effect, which is htmlspecialchars_decode().

Also just as simple is preventing possible SQL injection attacks by using PHP's mysql_real_escape_string function. This function works by escaping certain characters in any string. A malicious visitor may try to enter a SQL query into a form field in hopes that it will be executed. Look at the following example in which the visitor is trying to attempt to gain admin rights to the database by changing the database admin password. The hacker has also assumed some common words to try to determine table names:

```
UPDATE `user` SET `pwd`='gotcha!' WHERE `uid`='' OR `uid` LIKE
⟶  '%admin%'; --
```

If this SQL query was entered into the user name field, you could keep it from running by using `mysql_real_escape_string`:

```
$_POST['username'] = mysql_real_escape_string($_POST['username']);
```

This sets the value of `$_POST['username']` to:

```
UPDATE `user` SET `pwd`=\'gotcha!\' WHERE `uid`=\'\' or `uid` like
→ \'%admin%\'; --
```

Because the query is properly handled and certain characters are escaped, it is inserted into the database and will do no harm.

One other technique that you can use is securing the transmission of data between the client and the server. Let's focus on that next.

TRANSMITTING DATA SECURELY

Another option that you can consider is getting a security certificate for your site or application and then putting your site into an HTTPS security protocol. This is very useful because data traveling between the client and server cannot be read by potential attackers as easily, but it can be costly.

All of the Web site data is encrypted according to keys provided by the security certificate. The Web-site information is transmitted back and forth in a Secure Sockets Layer (SSL). The SSL is a cryptographic communications protocol for the Web. Once the data reaches either end of the transmission, it is decrypted properly for use. If you have used a Web site where the URL begins with `https://` or you have seen the lock icon on your Web browser, you have used a Web site protected in this manner. Many financial institutions and business Web sites use HTTPS to ensure that their data travels securely.

TIP: You can learn more about HTTPS and SSL at the Electronic Frontier Foundation's Web site at www.eff.org/https-everywhere.

WRAPPING **UP**

In this chapter, you learned how to combine jQuery AJAX shorthand methods like .get(), .post() and .load() with server-side scripting to add responsiveness to your HTML forms. Included in this chapter were methods for getting a response back from the server that you could process with jQuery to change page content or provide meaningful messages to your Web site visitors.

You were also introduced to the jQuery low-level AJAX methods that are used for more complex interactions with Web servers. Finally, you learned about JavaScript Object Notation (JSON) and how jQuery's JSON methods can be used to retrieve data from services like Twitter or Flickr for use on the Web sites that you will build.

If the first taste of a jQuery widget has left you hungry for more, you're in luck! Chapter 5, "Applying jQuery Widgets," explores widgets of all shapes and sizes, including several from the jQuery UI project. In addition to widgets from the jQuery UI project, you'll also learn about using plugins that others have developed and how to roll (and publish) your own plugins to share with others. Read on, Macduff!

5

APPLYING jQUERY WIDGETS

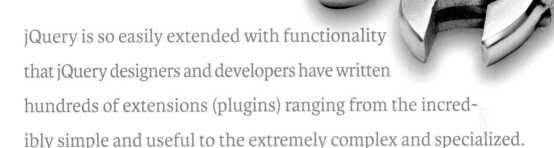

jQuery is so easily extended with functionality that jQuery designers and developers have written hundreds of extensions (plugins) ranging from the incredibly simple and useful to the extremely complex and specialized.

The jQuery UI (User Interface) library, a group of core plugins for interaction, widgets, and visual effects, continues to be developed as a separate branch of jQuery. Using the jQuery UI library will make your programming life much easier and provide you with the tools to add advanced features to your Web sites and applications effectively.

In this chapter, you'll learn about some very useful widgets from the jQuery UI, as well as some of the most effective and cool plugins made popular by the designer and developer community. In addition, I'll walk you through the steps to create your own plugins.

FIGURE 5.1 A portion of the ThemeRoller options available for configuring a custom style sheet to use with the jQuery UI widgets.

The jQuery UI is a complete library package to make interactive widgets come to life. A *widget* is a stand-alone package or tool that adds certain functionality—such as tabs or calendars from which you can pick dates—to your Web interfaces.

NOTE: Widgets are the components of the jQuery UI, whereas plugins is the term for developer-created and maintained widgets.

As an added bonus, you can download preconfigured styles, complete with images and icons, from the jQuery UI Web-site gallery (www.jqueryui.com). You can also roll your own CSS with the jQuery UI ThemeRoller, as shown in **Figure 5.1**.

CUSTOMIZING THE JQUERY UI

The jQuery UI ThemeRoller (available at http://jqueryui.com/themeroller) gives you the option of setting the CSS rules for the style sheet that will be downloaded with the jQuery UI library. The CSS rules set in the ThemeRoller are used to give the jQuery UI widgets the information they need to be visually integrated with your Web site.

Once you have picked a color palette for your Web site or application, it is easy to transfer that color palette and style information to the jQuery UI ThemeRoller (**Figure 5.2**). You can provide rules for the font settings, colors, and many of the individual elements that make up a jQuery UI widget. As you make the changes to each of the style rules in the ThemeRoller, the elements on the ThemeRoller page are updated automatically so that you can see the results of those changes immediately.

Once you have all of your style information set, you need to download the customized theme. When you click the Download theme button, you can select the jQuery UI widgets you want to include in your download. Some of the widgets that you can choose include:

- **Accordion.** Provides a widget with sliding content areas and is designed to provide a lot of content in a fixed space.

- **Autocomplete.** Attempts to predict words or phrases based on the input by a user.

- **Dialog.** Gives the developer a way to create interactive dialog boxes.

- **Tabs.** Provides a way to transform content containers into an interface resembling tabbed folders.

FIGURE 5.2 The jQuery UI ThemeRoller changes the styles of the elements as the information is entered into the ThemeRoller widget.

FIGURE 5.3 The location of the jQuery files and how they are referenced in the HTML files.

Be sure to take the time to read about and familiarize yourself with all of the widgets available from the jQuery UI Web site.

For now, download all of the widgets included in the jQuery UI library. In the future you can select just the widgets that you need for a particular project. Once you have configured the CSS theme to your liking, click Download. Your customized jQuery UI package will be presented to you as a compressed archive file in the ZIP format. Save the archive file to your hard drive.

Let's look at how to include the jQuery UI library in your HTML files next.

REFERENCING JQUERY UI FILES IN HTML FILES

When the archive file is safely on your hard drive, you can extract the files. It is important to note that the jQuery UI library contains lots of extra files that are not needed for your Web site, so do not transfer them to your Web server. **Figure 5.3** shows how I organize files for the most basic Web sites; highlighted are the files that you'll need from the jQuery UI download.

For the version of jQuery UI used in the Web site that will be developed in this chapter, I copied the *images* directory of the jQuery UI library download (and everything in it) and the jQuery UI CSS file *jquery-ui-1.8.12.custom.css* and then pasted them into the *chap5/css/ui* folder. The jQuery UI JavaScript file *jquery-ui-1.8.12.custom.min.js* is copied and pasted into the *chap5/inc/jQuery* folder. This will make the jQuery UI library files available to the Web site.

The jQuery UI files are then referenced properly in the HTML files that will use the jQuery UI widgets. Let's take it step by step and create a baseline file that will be added to as the chapter progresses.

1. Create a file called *5-0.php* and save it in the *chap5* folder.

2. Create the basic HTML layout for the site:

```
<!DOCTYPE html>
<html>
```

3. Create the opening head tag and include the basic character type and `title` of the page:

```
<head>
<meta http-equiv="Content-Type"
 → content="text/html; charset=UTF-8" />
<title>The Lodge at Mystic Forrest</title>
```

4. Reference the Web site's CSS and jQuery UI CSS files first:

```
<link type="text/css" rel="stylesheet"
 → href="css/lamf.css" />
<link type="text/css" rel="stylesheet"
 → href="css/ui/jquery-ui-1.8.12.custom.css" />
```

5. Load the jQuery and jQuery UI source files (take note of the order; the basic jQuery source must be loaded first):

```
<script type="text/javascript" src="inc/jQuery/jquery
 → -1.5.min.js"></script>
<script type="text/javascript"
 → src="inc/jQuery/jquery-ui-1.8.12.custom.min.js">
 → </script>
```

6. Provide a set of `script` tags and the document ready wrapper. You will include other jQuery calls in this wrapper:

```
<script type="text/javascript">
$(document).ready(function() {

});
</script>
```

7. Provide the remainder of the tags to complete the basic HTML layout.

```
</head>
<body>
</body>
</html>
```

With the jQuery UI in place, you can start adding some of the cool widgets that the jQuery UI provides for your Web site.

INCLUDING JQUERY UI WIDGETS

The jQuery UI widgets are well designed and easy to configure. In fact, the widgets are so well-designed that in some cases there is very little jQuery code to apply to your interfaces. Typically, you only have to call the widget and add the options required for your site.

It is more important that you apply the correct HTML markup when using the jQuery UI widgets. A good example of applying the proper markup is when you decide to build a tabbed interface. So, you'll do that next.

CREATING TABBED INTERFACES

One of the easiest ways to present content or multipart forms to Web-site visitors is with a tabbed interface. People are familiar with the concept of tabs as file folders, so navigating a Web site using tabs seems very natural. Web designers have been creating tabbed interfaces for years using complex CSS and JavaScript. The jQuery UI Tabs widget removes the complexity and adds some extremely flexible features for creating tabbed interfaces.

1. Open the basic file *chap5/5-0.php* and save it as *chap5/5-1.php* to set up the markup for the tabbed interface. In the body tag add a div for the header:

```
<body>
    <div id="header"></div>
```

2. Set up a div for the content area of the page:

```
<div id="content">
```

The tabs are defined by an unordered list. It is important that the anchor tags be preceded with a hash mark (highlighted) because the links will be used to reference any div added later:

```
<div id="contentTabs">
    <ul>
        <li><a href="#welcome">Welcome to the
        →  lodge...</a></li>
        <li><a href="#play">Play with us...</a></li>
        <li><a href="#stay">Stay with us...</a></li>
    </ul>
```

3. Set up a div for each tab and make sure that the id for each div matches the text entered into the anchor tags from the previous unordered list:

```
<div id="welcome">
        <h2>Mystic Forrest welcomes you...</h2>
</div>
<div id="play">
        <h2>Things to do...</h2>
</div>
<div id="stay">
        <h2>Make a reservation...</h2>
</div>
```

You can place almost any content that you want to in each div, as you will see when other jQuery UI widgets are added to the site.

4. Close out the div tags:

```
        </div>
    </div>
</body>
```

All that is left to do is add a bit of jQuery to turn your markup into tabs.

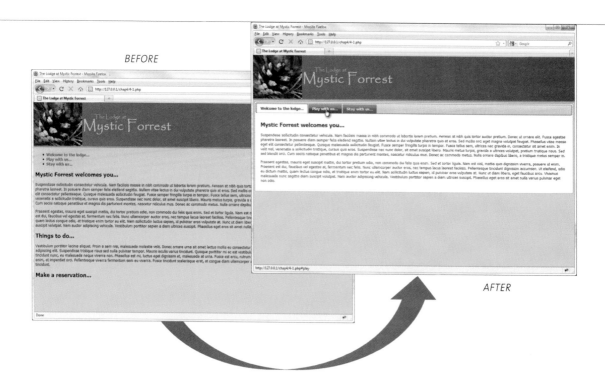

BEFORE

AFTER

FIGURE 5.4 The browser window before and after the addition of the jQuery UI Tabs widget.

5. In the head section of your markup add the highlighted code in the document ready wrapper:

```
<script type="text/javascript">
    $(document).ready(function() {
        $('#contentTabs').tabs();
    });
</script>
```

The jQuery UI takes care of manipulating the CSS for markup and browser events, turning your ordinary unordered list into a tabbed interface (**Figure 5.4**). By just following a few simple steps, the jQuery UI library eliminates hours of complex and tedious work.

That's it. One line of jQuery code with the proper supporting files and markup has transformed your ordinary Web site into an interactive masterpiece, and it was all made possible by the jQuery UI package.

The Tabs widget has many options available, including the ability to load content via AJAX. With the proper options set, you can even allow site visitors to rearrange the order of the tabs to suit their preferences.

Let's spice things up by giving users a way to select dates in forms.

ADDING CALENDARS TO FORMS

Instead of relying on site visitors to input dates correctly or having to write complex algorithms to parse dates entered by site visitors, it would be much easier if you had a tool that would allow users to select the dates they need to enter into forms. The jQuery UI provides just such a tool—the Datepicker.

Let's add a simple form to the "Stay with us" tab on the site that you are working on. This form gathers just enough information for the Web-site's owner to respond to site visitors about possible reservations at the site owner's small hotel.

1. Save a copy of the file you just completed, *chap5/5-1.php* as *chap5/5-2.php*.

2. Locate the div with an id of stay. Insert the following markup for a simple form:

```
<form name="reservationForm" method="post">
    <label class="formLabel" for="arrivalDate">Arrival Date:
    ➝ </label><input type="text" id="arrivalDate" /><br />
    <label class="formLabel" for="departureDate">Departure
    ➝ Date:</label><input type="text" id="departureDate"
    ➝ /><br />
    <label class="formLabel" for="visitorName">Visitor Name:
    ➝ </label><input type="text" id="visitorName" /><br />
    <label class="formLabel" for="phoneArea">Phone Number:
    ➝ </label>
    <input type="text" id="phoneArea" size="3" />
    <input type="text" id="phoneExchange" size="3" />
    <input type="text" id="phoneNumber" size="4" />
    <br />
    <label class="formLabel"> </label><button
    ➝ type="submit">Request Reservation</button><br />
    <label class="formLabel"> </label><button
    ➝ type="reset">Reset Form</button><br />
</form>
```

The jQuery code to handle both dates (`arrivalDate` and `departureDate`) is slightly more complex than the jQuery code for the tabs. Because the owner of the hotel only wants people to inquire about dates today or in the future, you need to set up the Datepicker with its `minDate` option. Then you'll need to employ Datepicker's `onSelect` option to set up the departure calendar so that only dates beyond the arrival date are available for selection.

3. Start the Datepicker function by binding the Datepicker to the form element that has an id of `arrivalDate`:

```
$('#arrivalDate').datepicker({
```

In many cases, options are passed to jQuery UI widgets and the plugins that you will learn about later in the form of an object. As you learned in Chapter 4, JavaScript objects are specified in *object literal notation*, in other words *name: value* pairs.

4. You do not want dates in the past to be available for the user to select. So, set the `minDate` option to 0 to set the earliest selectable date to today (**Figure 5.5**):

```
minDate: 0,
```

Once a date has been selected for the arrival, you can use the `onSelect` option of the Datepicker to create a date value that occurs beyond the arrival date. The site owner does not want the visitor to be able to select a departure date that occurs before the arrival date.

5. Open the `onSelect` option and pass the selected date in the `dateText` variable:

```
onSelect: function(dateText) {
```

6. Begin the calculation of a proper departure date by converting the `dateText` variable to a real date with JavaScript's Date function:

```
var depart = new Date(dateText);
```

7. Set the date contained in the `depart` variable to one day greater than the value it currently holds (which happens to be the arrival date despite what it is called):

```
depart.setDate(depart.getDate()+1);
```

FIGURE 5.5 Users cannot click a date earlier than today, provided that today is July 19, 2011, in this case.

FIGURE 5.6 The Datepicker's minimum departure date is one day greater than the arrival date.

8. Bind the datepicker to the form input element with an `id` of `departureDate` and set the `minDate` option to the new potential departure date:

```
$('#departureDate').datepicker({
    minDate: depart
});
```

9. Close up the function with the appropriate braces and parentheses:

```
    }
});
```

Once complete, the departure date is set to be a minimum date of the day after the arrival date (**Figure 5.6**).

As with other jQuery UI widgets, the Datepicker provides a wide array of options for customizing the widget, including animations, the ability to show multiple months at once, and the capability to localize the calendar to certain regions with the proper language choice in place.

After the Datepicker is added to the form and configured with the options that you desire, you can submit the form using AJAX. Let's set that up next and use the jQuery UI Dialog widget to give site visitors a chance to confirm their submission.

ESTABLISHING A "DIALOG" WITH VISITORS

Part of the interaction that you can establish with users of your Web site or application is provided in the form of dialog boxes. You can use dialog boxes to inform or warn your users. You can also use them to gather additional information from users, even if that information is as simple as confirming a form submission.

The jQuery UI Dialog widget is very flexible and offers a number of options for customization. Let's set up a dialog box to confirm submission of the reservation request. There are several pieces to setting up even a simple dialog box; they include HTML, PHP, and jQuery. To provide the interaction, you'll set up each of the pieces, beginning with the HTML, next.

1. Open *chap5/5-2.php* and save a copy of it as *chap5/5-3.php*.

2. Prior to the closing body tag in the HTML, add the following lines of markup to establish the markup for the dialog box:

   ```
   <div id="dialog" title="Verify Submission">
       <p>Are you sure you wish to inquire about these dates?</p>
   </div>
   ```

   Because this will be a simple confirmation dialog box, the HTML is very simple. The title attribute in the div tag will be used for the title of the dialog box, whereas the content of the div will be used in the body of the dialog box.

3. Run the SQL file *chap5/sql/lodge.sql* (available in the code download) on your database package to set up the database and create the table that will hold the reservation requests.

   Now that the HTML markup is complete and the database table is established, you can turn your attention to creating the PHP code for handling the reservation inquiry.

4. Create *chap5/inc/**reserve.php*** and set up the connection to the database. Be sure to use the correct user name and password for the database connection:

```
if(!$dbc = mysql_connect('localhost', 'username', 'password')){
    echo 'error connecting to the database('.mysql_errno().'):
    ⇢ '.mysql_error() . "\n";
    exit();
}
```

5. Add a sleep function to the process. The sleep function will cause the program to hesitate for the defined time before performing the next line of code (the requirement of adding a sleep statement will become clear in the section "Informing users with a Progressbar"). Set it up for 2 seconds:

```
sleep(2);
```

6. Create the SQL statement that will be used to place the information from an AJAX post request into the reserverequests table:

```
$reserveIN = "INSERT INTO `lamf`.`reserverequests` ";

$reserveIN .= "(`arrival`, `departure`, `guest`, `phone`) ";

$reserveIN .= "VALUES (";

$reserveIN .= "'".mysql_real_escape_string($_POST
⇢ ['arrivalDate'])."', ";

$reserveIN .= "'".mysql_real_escape_string($_POST
⇢ ['departureDate'])."', ";

$reserveIN .= "'".mysql_real_escape_string($_POST
⇢ ['visitorName'])."', ";

$reserveIN .= "'".mysql_real_escape_string($_POST
⇢ ['phoneArea']).'-'.mysql_real_escape_string($_POST
⇢ ['phoneExchange']).'-'.mysql_real_escape_string($_POST
⇢ ['phoneNumber'])."' ";

$reserveIN .= ")";
```

7. Run the SQL statement on the database and report any errors:

```
if(!($reservation = mysql_query($reserveIN, $dbc))){
    echo mysql_errno();
    exit();
}
```

For this form, the AJAX process does not need or expect any return from the database, so no information is returned from the query other than any error that may occur. This completes the PHP, leaving you free to move on to the jQuery script.

The jQuery script has two functions, one bound to the form's Submit button that will call the dialog function and the dialog function itself.

1. Open *chap5/5-3.php* and locate the document ready function in the head section of the HTML.

2. Start the dialog process by binding a submit method to the reservation form:

```
$('#reservationForm').submit(function(e){
```

3. Call the jQuery UI Dialog open method on the HTML markup you created earlier in this exercise:

```
$('#dialog').dialog('open');
```

4. Apply the preventDefault method to the submit event and close the function:

```
e.preventDefault();
});
```

5. For usage in this site, add one other dialog method bound to the div element you created in the HTML earlier:

```
$('#dialog').dialog({
```

6. Add the autoOpen option first. By setting this option to false, you keep the dialog box from opening until the dialog open method is called:

```
autoOpen: false,
```

7. Set the width of the dialog box:

```
width: 325,
```

8. Set the `modal` option to `true` if you want the dialog box to have the properties that a modal window has (a shaded background through which you can see other content but helps the user to focus on the interaction at hand):

```
modal: true,
```

9. Set the `resizable` option to `false`. For the dialog box to be used in this situation there is no need to make it resizable:

```
resizable: false,
```

Next, you need to create the buttons for the dialog box. In the dialog box the question, "Are you sure you wish to inquire about these dates?" is presented to the user. The possible answers are YES or NO. Each button will fire its own functions.

10. Create the first button, the YES button:

```
buttons: {
    "YES": function() {
```

11. The jQuery UI Dialog buttons have callback functions available to them. So, within the callback, `serialize` the form and use jQuery's AJAX post method to send the serialized data to the PHP handler script *chap5/inc/ reserve.php* that you created earlier:

```
var formData = $('#reservationForm').serialize();
$.post('inc/reserve.php', formData);
```

Because there is no data to be returned from the `post` method, there is no callback assigned to the AJAX function.

12. Clear the text inputs of the form to give users an indication that something has happened:

```
$('#reservationForm input[type="text"]').val('');
```

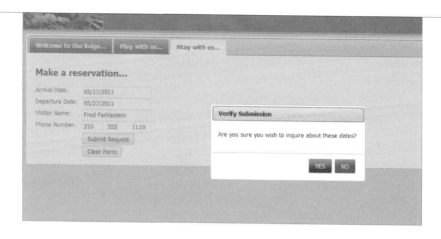

FIGURE 5.7 The jQuery UI dialog box is set up to act as a confirmation interaction.

13. Call the `dialog close` method on the dialog box after the YES button has been clicked and the AJAX call has been performed:

```
$(this).dialog("close");
```

14. For the NO button on the dialog box, there isn't any functionality required, so close the dialog box:

```
}, "NO": function() {
    $(this).dialog("close");
}
```

15. Add the closing brackets for the `dialog` function:

```
    }
});
```

16. Navigate to the "Stay with us" tab, fill out the form, and then click Submit. The jQuery UI Dialog widget box pops up and offers you the option of submitting the dates (**Figure 5.7**).

The interaction provided by the jQuery UI Dialog widget works well, but it could leave users wondering if anything occurred. The data was removed from the form very abruptly, and the dialog box disappeared. Users might be more comforted if they see and perceive that an action is taking place. And that sounds like a perfect job for the jQuery UI Progressbar!

INFORMING USERS WITH A PROGRESSBAR

Using a jQuery UI Progressbar widget to give users a visual cue that a process is occurring can be as simple or as complex as you want to make it. In some cases, you can simply just display an animated Progressbar to indicate to users that an action is occurring. In other instances, you can set up a complex interaction with the jQuery UI Progressbar widget that will allow it to accept incremental information from certain operations that you can then use to move the bar from left to right.

AJAX requests do not return the kind of incremental information that you would need to perform this movement, because AJAX requests are asynchronous. You can either guess at the incremental values (not recommended), or you can find other ways to use the jQuery UI Progressbar widget to get the desired result.

> **NOTE:** AJAX does not typically return any information to the browser until the XMLHttpRequest is complete (refer to Chapter 4). You can force the browser to return incremental information via the AJAX request, but it is a very complex process and in some cases may cause the user's browser to "lock up" until the request is complete.

One way to use the jQuery UI Progressbar widget is having it display an animated image to indicate action. That is the method you'll use here.

You'll show the jQuery UI Progressbar in a modal window using techniques that you learned earlier. Once confirmation about submitting the date information is received, the Progressbar will be invoked in the ajaxStart function. After the AJAX request has completed, the Progressbar will fade out and then disappear.

1. To configure the CSS for the jQuery UI Progressbar and modal window, open *chap5/css/lamf.css* and insert the shade property:

    #progressShade {

2. Hide the shade initially by setting its display property to none:

        display: none;

3. Set the color and position of the shade:

```
background: #323232;
position: fixed;
left: 0;
top: 0;
```

4. Configure the height and width along with the z-index of the shade:

```
width: 100%;
height: 100%;
z-index: 100;
}
```

5. Set up the CSS rules for the element that will hold the jQuery UI Progressbar widget:

```
#progressbar {
```

6. Hide the Progressbar until it is needed:

```
display: none;
```

7. Configure the position, height, and width:

```
position: fixed;
height: 12px;
width: 200px;
```

8. Set the correct margin and position data to center the jQuery UI Progressbar widget on the browser window:

```
margin: auto;
top: 50%;
left: 50%;
```

9. Set the z-index to a number high enough to ensure that it will appear on *top* of every other element:

```
z-index: 200;
}
```

Now you need to prepare the jQuery to display the jQuery UI Progressbar widget.

1. Save a copy of *chap5/5-3.php* as *chap5/5-4.php*.

2. Bind ajaxStart to the body:

   ```
   $('body').ajaxStart(function() {
   ```

3. Using the same techniques demonstrated earlier in the book for setting up modal windows, add the modal window code into the ajaxStart function.

   ```
   $('body').append('<div id="progressbar"></div>
   →  <div id="progressShade"></div>');
   var modalMarginTop = ($('#progressbar').height()) / 2;
   var modalMarginLeft = ($('#progressbar').width()) / 2;
   $('#progressbar').css({
       'margin-top' : -modalMarginTop,
       'margin-left' : -modalMarginLeft
   });
   $('#progressShade').css('opacity', '0.4');
   ```

4. Call the jQuery UI Progressbar widget within the ajaxStart function:

   ```
   $( "#progressbar" ).progressbar({
   ```

5. Initialize the Progressbar's value option to 100. This means that the bar will be fully extended from left to right in the space that it occupies on the Web page:

   ```
   value: 100
   });
   ```

6. Fade in the Progressbar with the animated image, giving the appearance that an action is occurring:

   ```
   $('#progressbar, #progressShade').fadeIn(250);
   });
   ```

FIGURE 5.8 The jQuery UI Progressbar widget indicates to users that a process is running.

7. Remove the jQuery UI Progressbar widget during the ajaxStop function after the AJAX request is completed:

```
$('body').ajaxStop(function() {
    $('#progressbar, #progressShade').fadeOut(400, function(){
        $('#progressbar, #progressShade').remove();
    });
});
```

Under normal circumstances, the AJAX request and response cycle that drives the appearance and removal of the jQuery UI Progressbar widget in the Web site would happen so quickly that the Progressbar would barely have time to appear before it faded away. This is the reason the sleep function was placed into the PHP file in the section "Establishing a 'dialog' with visitors." The sleep function pads the request with a small amount of time that gives the Progressbar a longer screen life. **Figure 5.8** shows the Progressbar in action.

Giving users visual clues in the manner that the jQuery UI Progressbar widget does is a valuable method for keeping Web-site visitors engaged. Web application users appreciate knowing that they have some amount of control over their inter-action with the application.

Another method that you can use to keep users engaged is the jQuery UI Auto-complete widget. Let's look at a way to use that widget next.

COMPLETING FIELDS AUTOMATICALLY

Blind searches where the user enters information into a form and clicks a button to await the results are nearly history on the Internet today. Many Web sites, includ-ing large sites like Google, are opting to provide users with immediate suggestions based on what users type into an input field.

The jQuery UI Autocomplete widget gives you the power to accomplish imme-diate suggestion functionality easily. Let's add this widget to the Web site next.

1. Open *chap5/5-4.php* and save a copy of it as *chap5/5-5.php*. Locate the HTML markup for the second tab. That markup is in the div with an id of play.

2. Set up the only markup needed to support the jQuery UI Autocomplete widget, a form input box:

```
<div id="play">
    <h2>Things to do...</h2>
    <div id="widget">
        <label for="attractions">Attractions: </label>
        <input type="text" id="attractions" size="32" />
    </div>
```

3. Set up a div to hold the results of the search:

```
        <div id="attractionInfo"></div>
</div>
```

You'll create the jQuery script for the Autocomplete widget in a separate file called *chap5/inc/jQuery/attractions.js*.

4. Make sure you include the following line to reference that file in the head section of *5-5.php*:

```
<script type="text/javascript"
→  src="inc/jQuery/attractions.js"></script>
```

5. To configure the jQuery script file, *chap5/inc/jQuery/attractions.js*, build an array of attractions:

```
$(function(){
    var attractions = [
            "Admiral Nimitz Museum - Fredericksburg",
            "Aquarena Springs Nature Center - San Marcos",
            "Canyon Lake - Sattler",
            "Dinosaur Flats - Startzville",
            "Enchanted Rock - Fredericksburg",
            "Gruene Hall - New Braunfels",
            "Guadalupe River State Park - Spring Branch",
            "Live Oak Disc Golf Course - Live Oak",
            "Longhorn Caverns - Boerne",
            "Lost Maples State Park - Vanderpool",
            "National Museum of the Pacific War - Fredericksburg",
            "Wonder World - San Marcos"
    ];
```

6. Bind the autocomplete method to the input text box that was created earlier:

```
$('#attractions').autocomplete({
```

7. Provide the Autocomplete widget with a reference to the source of the data to be used to perform the job of presenting immediate suggestions to the user. The source here is the array that was completed, called `attractions`:

```
source: attractions,
```

8. Place the text for the selected item, returned in `ui.item`, into the variable `selectedAttraction`:

```
select: function(event, ui) {
    var selectedAttraction = ui.item.value;
```

9. Split the `selectedAttraction` variable into an array using the JavaScript split method. The first word of the array, `arrayAttractName`, is used to identify the element in *chap5/inc/attractionInfo.php* that will be retrieved:

FIGURE 5.9 As a user starts to type in a search term, the suggested search terms are returned by Autocomplete.

```
var arrayAttractionName =
→ selectedAttraction.split(' ');
```

10. Load the information about the attraction into the element having the `id` of `attractionInfo`:

```
$('#attractionInfo').load('inc/attractionInfo.php
→ #'+arrayAttractionName[0]);
    }
  });
});
```

The progression of the jQuery UI Autocomplete widget is shown in **Figure 5.9**.

The core widgets of the jQuery UI library really do provide a lot of additional functionality in a small and easily usable package. However, these widgets only scratch the surface of what is available to you as a designer or developer for adding interaction via jQuery to your Web applications.

Let's continue to examine widgets that you can add to your sites that are available from other developers just like you.

NOTE: The file containing the information about the attractions, chap5/inc/attractionInfo.php, was created with only a couple of attractions for demonstration purposes.

USING **jQUERY PLUGINS**

As mentioned previously, the development community embraced and extended jQuery by adding, and continuing to add, hundreds of plugins. Members of the community make these plugins available for other designers and developers in the community to use in their own sites and applications, and the plugins are usually free of any charges or royalties.

The jQuery team acknowledges this effort and has included space on its Web site at http://plugins.jquery.com to feature these plugins. On the Web site you can find listings for plugins from AJAX to widgets.

Sorting through these plugins to determine some of the most useful was quite a trick due to the sheer volume of plugins available. In the end, I chose several plugins that you'll be able to put to work quickly and easily in your Web applications and on your Web sites:

- **Tablesorter.** Gives you the capability to add sorting functions to any ordinary HTML table.

- **TinyTips.** A tool tip generator that allows you to add further information to almost any element.

- **gMap.** Makes interacting with Google's map API straightforward and provides you with a wide range of options to give you the ability to deliver extensive information to your Web-site visitors via maps.

- **jqPlot.** A powerful plugin that will give you the power to present complex data to your visitors in plot and graph form.

> **NOTE:** Developers who provide plugins put a lot of hard work and time into making their products easy to use and free of charge for the Web-site designer and developer community. To support the developers and the continued development of their plugins, I encourage you to donate to these people who help to simplify your job, and mine. (Many plugin Web sites have links on them that allow you to donate to the developer.)

BEEFING UP YOUR APPS WITH PLUGINS

When developing Web sites and applications, you'll turn to certain tools over and over again to accomplish specific effects or provide particular kinds of content. The jQuery plugins discussed in the following sections fit that bill. In addition to providing easy access to certain kinds of content, these jQuery plugins are simple to use and add value to the content that you present to your Web-site visitors.

One of the actions that computer users have always appreciated is the ability to sort a data-filled table by one or more columns. Sorting tables helps users to make sense of the data and provides them a way to mine the data for trends.

You can extend this action to your Web-based tables by adding the jQuery Tablesorter plugin.

SORTING TABLE RECORDS

Christian Bach's Tablesorter plugin (available from http://tablesorter.com/docs) is the most efficient plugin available for adding sort capabilities to any HTML table. So, let's incorporate it into the lodge Web site.

In the lodge example, the owner wants to see and respond to all of the reservation requests. Because these requests come in with different dates that might not be in order, the lodge owner needs to be able to sort the records and respond to the requests that will come up first.

1. Open *chap5/5-5.php* and save a copy of it as *chap5/**5-6.php**.*

2. Start writing the PHP that will get the list of reservation requests, beginning with the database connection (make sure you use the username and password you have set up for your database):

```php
<?php
if(!$dbc = mysql_connect('localhost', username, 'password')){
    echo mysql_error() . "\n";
    exit();
}
```

3. Add the very simple query to get the data from the table:

```php
$getRequests = "SELECT `arrival`,`departure`,`guest`,`phone` ";
$getRequests .= "FROM `lamf`.`reserverequests` ";
```

```
$getRequests .= "WHERE `response` = '' ";

if(!($requests = mysql_query($getRequests, $dbc))){

    echo mysql_errno();

    exit();

}

?>
```

The PHP will retrieve all of the reservation requests records from the database.

4. Create the HTML section of the page, including the Tablesorter CSS file. Make sure that the Tablesorter plugin script is included after the basic jQuery file:

```
<!DOCTYPE html>

<html>

    <head>

    <meta http-equiv="Content-Type" content="text/html;
    → charset=UTF-8" />

    <title>The Lodge at Mystic Forrest</title>

        <link type="text/css" rel="stylesheet"
        → href="css/lamf.css" />

        <link type="text/css" rel="stylesheet"
        → href="css/ui/jquery-ui-1.8.12.custom.css" />

        <link type="text/css" rel="stylesheet"
        → href="css/tablesorter/style.css" />

        <script type="text/javascript" src="inc/jQuery/jquery
        → -1.5.min.js"></script>

        <script type="text/javascript"
        → src="inc/jQuery/jquery-ui-1.8.12.custom.min.js">
        → </script>

        <script type="text/javascript"
        → src="inc/jQuery/jquery.tablesorter.min.js">
        → </script>
```

5. Bind the Tablesorter method to a table with an id of requests:

```
<script type="text/javascript">
$(document).ready(function() {
    $('#requests').tablesorter({
```

The jQuery Tablesorter plugin has a number of options available, but only one is called here. The Responded column in the table doesn't need to be sortable. Columns are counted left to right beginning with zero; the Responded column is number four.

6. Set the Responded column's sorter property to false:

```
headers: {4:{sorter: false}}
});
```

7. Close out the script.

```
});
</script>
</head>
```

The function is now ready to perform.

8. Create the body of the HTML markup. Call a PHP script from within the HTML to set up the table to be sorted:

```
<body>
<div id="header"></div>
<div id="content">
<h2>Reservation Requests</h2>
```

9. Create a conditional check in the PHP section to test if there is data in the table; if not, the PHP code will return a message that there is no data available so that the user doesn't perceive that there might be something wrong with this application:

```
<?php
if(0 != mysql_num_rows($requests)){
```

10. If there is data, begin the HTML table output. Make sure that the table has an id of requests (that is the id the tablesorter method is bound to in this example) and give it a class of tablesorter to enable CSS styling:

```
echo '<table id="requests" class="tablesorter">';
```

11. The jQuery Tablesorter plugin requires that the table have both a properly formed thead section and tbody section. Set up the thead section with the proper column names:

```
echo '<thead>';
echo '<tr><th>Arrival Date</th><th>Departure
→ Date</th><th>Guest Name</th><th>Guest
→ Phone</th><th>Responded</th></tr>';
echo '</thead>';
```

12. Turn your attention to the tbody section. Set up the PHP to loop through all of the records and place the information into the proper table cells:

```
echo '<tbody>';
while($pendingRequest =
→ mysql_fetch_array($requests)){
    echo '<tr class="even">';
    echo '<td>'.$pendingRequest['arrival'].
    → '</td>';
    echo '<td>'.$pendingRequest['departure'].
    → '</td>';
    echo '<td>'.$pendingRequest['guest'].'</td>';
    echo '<td>'.$pendingRequest['phone'].'</td>';
    echo '<td><input type="checkbox"
    → name="response[]" /></td>';
    echo '</tr>';
}
```

13. Close out the tbody section and table:

```
echo '</tbody>';
echo '</table>';
```

14. Provide a message to the user if there is no data returned by the query:

```
} else {
    echo '<p>There are no pending reservation
    →  requests</p>';
}
?>
```

15. Put the rest of the HTML tags into place. **Figure 5.10** shows the completed table.

```
    </div>
  </body>
</html>
```

The records are sorted in the order in which they were input into the database. In this table four columns, Arrival Date, Departure Date, Guest Name, and Guest Phone, are sortable. **Figure 5.11** shows the sorting action that occurs when you click on the header for Arrival Date.

NOTE: I purposely omitted how users can remove a record from being displayed in the table by selecting the check box in the column Responded. A good exercise would be to add the jQuery *change* event to the check boxes and use jQuery's AJAX functionality to mark that record as responded to. Then users will only have to view the records they need to respond to.

No matter how simple or complex your tables may be, the Tablesorter plugin will provide you with many options to ensure that your Web-site users can sort data to their heart's content.

Another way of providing additional information is supplying a tool tip when the mouse hovers over an element in your HTML page. Let's add a tool-tip plugin to the site that will provide additional information about the tabs.

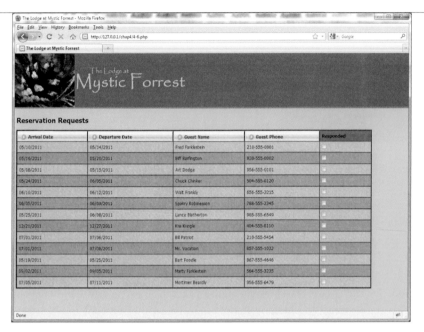

FIGURE 5.10 The freshly loaded table with the data unsorted.

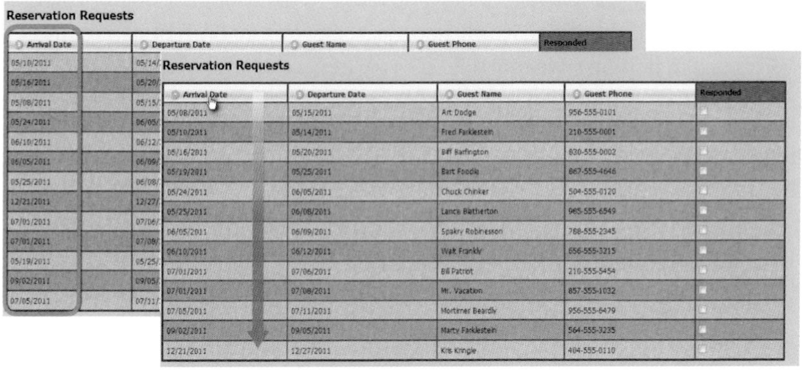

FIGURE 5.11 The first column is ordered from earliest arrival date to latest arrival date.

PROVIDING BITE-SIZED INFORMATION

Tool tips, such as the one shown in **Figure 5.12**, can be a great way to present your Web-site visitors with additional information about a link or a word on a Web page.

The jQuery TinyTips plugin (available at www.mikemerritt.me/blog/jquery-plugin-tinytips-1-1 and authored by Mike Merritt) is a small, easy-to-use, and extremely flexible plugin that will give you the option of presenting pictures as well as text in pop-up style tool tips. Let's try it!

1. Open *chap5/5-6.php* and save a copy of it as *chap5/5-7.php*. Insert the source references for the TinyTips CSS and jQuery script files in the head section (highlighted):

```
<link type="text/css" rel="stylesheet" href="css/lamf.css" />

<link type="text/css" rel="stylesheet"
→ href="css/ui/jquery-ui-1.8.12.custom.css" />

<link type="text/css" rel="stylesheet"
→ href="css/tinyTips/tinyTips.css" />

<script type="text/javascript"
→ src="inc/jQuery/jquery-1.5.min.js"></script>

<script type="text/javascript"
→ src="inc/jQuery/jquery-ui-1.8.12.custom.min.js"></script>
```

```
<script type="text/javascript"
→  src="inc/jQuery/attractions.js"></script>

<script type="text/javascript"
→  src="inc/jQuery/jquery.tinyTips.js"></script>
```

2. Locate the `$(document).ready(function() {` ... section of the code between the head tags and include the following jQuery to set up the TinyTips:

```
$('a.tinyTip').tinyTips('yellow', 'title');
```

You are binding the anchor tags with a `class` of `tinyTip` to the `tinyTips` method. The properties in the `tinyTips` method are (in order) the CSS styles to use and the element attribute that will be displayed in the tool tip.

3. To create TinyTips on a couple of the tabs on the lodge's Web site, include the class `tinyTip` and add a title attribute to the HTML markup for the tabs:

```
<ul>
    <li><a href="#welcome" title="Welcome to Mystic Forrest">
→   Welcome to the lodge...</a></li>

    <li><a href="#play" class="tinyTip" title="Find Area
→   Attractions">Play with us...</a></li>

    <li><a href="#stay" class="tinyTip" title="Make a
→   Reservation Request">Stay with us...</a></li>
</ul>
```

Be sure to visit the TinyTips plugin Web site for other options and ways to use TinyTips in your Web sites and applications.

While you're adding more information for the lodge site visitors, it would make sense to provide them with map information, which many business Web sites do. Due to the popularity of featuring map data on Web sites, Google has provided an API that you can use to interact with its map application. The next jQuery plugin, gMap, gives you the tools that you need to use the Google Maps API easily and effectively in your Web sites.

PUTTING BUSINESS ON THE MAP

The number of Web sites that use the Google Maps API to display maps of various types is staggering. Web sites use maps to provide directions, highlight all of their locations, and even guide players in live, interactive games.

There is only one problem: The Google Maps API can be a bear to use, especially when all a designer wants to do is include a map to show the location of a retailer or service.

Cedric Kastner eliminated the complexity with his jQuery plugin for Google maps, which he called gMap (download it from http://gmap.nurtext.de). The only requirement for using gMap, other than including the proper files in your markup, is that you have an account with Google so that you can sign up for a Google Maps API key. You can sign up for the key at http://code.google.com/intl/en-US/apis/maps/signup.html.

Let's put the lodge's location on the map.

1. Save a copy of *chap5/5-7.php* as *chap5/5-8.php*. Make sure you include the gMap plugin source file in the head section of *chap5/5-8.php*, just as you did with the plugin files you used earlier.

2. Include the following script reference using your Google Maps API key in the head section (add this before the reference to the gMap script):

    ```
    <script type="text/javascript"
      src="http://maps.google.com/maps?file=api&amp;v=2&amp;
      key=YOUR_API_KEY_GOES_HERE"></script>
    ```

3. Add the following style rules and properties in your CSS file *chap5/css/lamf.css*. These properties will be used to define the container for the map:

    ```
    #lodgeMap {
        position: relative;
    ```

4. Define a height and width for the element used to hold the map:

    ```
        width: 700px;
        height: 450px;
    ```

5. Center the element that holds the map on the screen:

```
    margin-left: -350px;
    left: 50%;
}
```

6. Add the jQuery code for the gMap plugin to the document ready wrapper in the head section of the HTML file, *chap5/5-8.php*. Bind the gMap plugin to the element that will hold the map:

```
<script type="text/javascript">
    $(document).ready(function(){
        $('#lodgeMap').gMap({
```

7. Set your gMap options. Place a marker at a certain latitude and longitude:

```
            markers: [{
                latitude: 29.871266,
                longitude: -98.237708
            }],
```

8. Pass the type of map and zoom level to the gMap plugin:

```
            maptype: G_PHYSICAL_MAP,
            zoom: 12
        });
    });
</script>
```

The maptype: G_PHYSICAL_MAP option provides a terrain view on the map (**Figure 5.13**).

9. Add the element to hold the map somewhere in the HTML body:

```
<div id="lodgeMap"></div>
```

10. Load the page.

The jQuery gMap plugin presents the map centered on the location entered complete with a marker and zoomed in at such a level as to provide some detail about the terrain to users. Again, be sure to check the gMap Web site for many more options that were not demonstrated here.

Plotting points on a map and plotting information in a chart are easy when using jQuery plugins. To make data reporting more intuitive, it is often desirable to present that information graphically as bar or pie charts, or along plot and trend lines. The next plugin, jqPlot, provides a thorough library for providing these types of charts to your Web-application users.

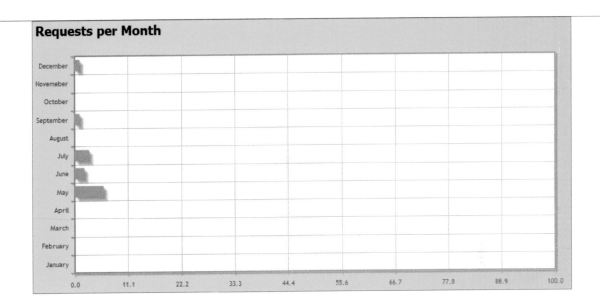

PLOTTING AND CHARTING DATA

Up to this point, the plugins have been fairly simple to use. Chris Leonello's jqPlot plugin is no different (available at www.jqplot.com) in its simplicity. What is different is the volume of options available to you for creating and customizing many types of graphs and charts. This kind of flexibility comes at a price: You must be meticulous in how you set up the display and data details when using this plugin.

In this example, you'll create a bar chart (**Figure 5.14**) to show the lodge owner the number of reservation requests per month that come through the Web site. You'll add the chart to the page where the lodge owner sees the reservation requests that need to be processed.

Start the exercise by modifying the site's CSS file.

1. Open *chap5/css/lamf.css* and add a height and width property to the CSS selector requestChart. This selector will be connected to the element in the HTML where the chart is to be displayed:

```
#requestChart {
    width: 800px;
    height: 350px;
}
```

To retrieve the data from the database and format the data properly for use by the jQuery jqPlot plugin, the PHP must be crafted very carefully. jqPlot expects a label (in the form of a numerical index value) and a value to be plotted on the chart in pairs using JavaScript Object Notation (JSON):

```
[0,1],[0,2],[0,3],[0,4],[6,5],[2,6],[3,7],[0,8],[1,9],[0,10],
   [0,11],[1,12]
```

The first number in each pair represents the value to be plotted. The second value is the plot index (in this case matched to a month of the year).

TIP: Many jQuery plugins use data configured as JSON based on its being a subset of JavaScript's object literal notation. This helps to keep notation consistent from plugin to plugin and helps the developer avoid having to learn different formats for passing information to plugins.

The PHP request to the MySQL database will use the same connection that was created earlier; let's look at the code you'll add to the PHP section of the page.

2. Save a copy of chap5/5-8.php as chap5/5-9.php. This is the file you will add the additional PHP and jQuery code to for displaying the bar graph.

3. Declare a variable in the PHP section of 5-9.php that will hold the plot data from the database immediately after the database query is done:

```
$ra = '';
```

4. Create an array called requestArray that will be used to index the database request:

```
$requestArray = array(1,2,3,4,5,6,7,8,9,10,11,12);
```

5. Loop through the $requestArray and start making requests to the database based on the $requestArray:

```
for($i = 0; $i < count($requestArray); $i++){
    $getReservationsByMonth = "SELECT count(*) as reqCount
       FROM `lamf`.`reserverequests` WHERE SUBSTRING
       (`arrival`, 1, 2) = ".$requestArray[$i];
```

6. Run the query. The query returns any errors that occur:

```
if(!($requestsMonth =
   → mysql_query($getReservationsByMonth, $dbc))){
     echo mysql_errno();
     exit();
}
```

7. To make sure that the JSON array string is formatted properly, insert a comma between each bracketed pair of values. If the value of $i is less than 11 (December), insert the comma (highlighted):

```
if($i < 11){
     $ra .= '['. mysql_result($requestsMonth, 0)
     → .','. ($i+1) . '],';
```

PHP's mysql_result returns the first item (the count of requests made in the given month) from the query $requestsMonth. Because the index of the $requestArray is actually one less than the actual numerical index of the month (remember that PHP array indexes start with zero), you add 1 to that value to make sure the months line up properly.

8. Eliminate the possibility of putting a comma after the pair if the month is December ($i == 11):

```
} else {
     $ra .= '['. mysql_result($requestsMonth, 0)
     → .','. ($i+1) . ']';
}
}
```

Now that the PHP is outputting the proper data format, you can focus your attention on inserting the right files to be referenced in the head section of the HTML. The jqPlot plugin has several optional add-ons, and depending on the chart you expect to display, you may have to include any number of these add-ons.

9. Make sure that you reference jqPlot's CSS style sheet:

```
<link type="text/css" rel="stylesheet" href="css/jqPlot/
↪ jquery.jqplot.css" />
```

10. For bar charts, a couple of the jqPlot add-ons are needed. The first add-on is not required for Microsoft's Internet Explorer 9 but is needed for earlier versions of Internet Explorer. The add-on is called within a CSS conditional comment (all add-ons are included after the base file for jqPlot):

```
<script type="text/javascript"
↪ src="inc/jQuery/jquery.jqplot.min.js"></script>

<!--[if lt IE 9]><script type="text/javascript"
↪ src="inc/jQuery/excanvas.min.js"></script><![endif]-->
```

11. For bar charts and charts where text will be used along either axis of the chart, you must reference the *jqplot.barRenderer.min.js* and *jqplot. categoryAxisRenderer.min.js* files:

```
<script type="text/javascript"
↪ src="inc/jQuery/jqplot.barRenderer.min.js"></script>

<script type="text/javascript"
↪ src="inc/jQuery/jqplot.categoryAxisRenderer.min.js">
↪ </script>
```

12. Write the jQuery to display the chart. Enable jqPlot's add-ons:

```
$.jqplot.config.enablePlugins = true;
```

13. Get the data from the PHP function and insert it into the JavaScript variable line1:

```
line1 = [<?php echo $ra; ?>];
```

14. Call the jqplot function. Bind the function to the element where the chart will be displayed and provide the data contained in the variable line1:

```
$.jqplot('requestChart', [line1], {
```

15. Declare the $.jqplot.BarRenderer add-on as part of the seriesDefaults option. This is done in order to display a bar chart:

```
seriesDefaults: {

    renderer: $.jqplot.BarRenderer,
```

jqPlot now knows the chart renderer add-on that will be used.

16. Set the options for the renderer, a barDirection of horizontal and a barMargin of 10:

```
rendererOptions: {

    barDirection: 'horizontal',

    barMargin: 5

    }

},
```

The barMargin option sets the spacing between the bars. **Figure 5.15** shows bars with a zero margin; the overlap doesn't look good.

Next you'll set up the details for each axis of the chart, beginning with the y-axis. The y-axis will show the Month names.

17. Set the renderer for the y-axis:

```
axes: {

    yaxis: {

        renderer: $.jqplot.CategoryAxisRenderer,
```

18. Provide the information for the ticks option, in this case the names of the months:

```
ticks: ['January', 'February', 'March',
→  'April', 'May', 'June', 'July',
→  'August', 'September', 'October',
→  'November', 'December']

},
```

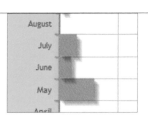

FIGURE 5.15 A margin of zero causes each bar to fill up the available space and may make the chart hard to read.

19. Provide the information for the x-axis of the chart. The lodge owner believes he'll get about 100 requests via his Web site per month. Configure the x-axis to start with a minimum of zero requests and a maximum of 100 requests:

```
xaxis: {min: 0, max: 100, numberTicks:11}
    }
});
```

20. Designate 11 ticks along the x-axis to display ten evenly proportioned columns (**Figure 5.16**).

If you need to create complex dashboards—displaying charts and graphs of various types—to report on various elements of your enterprise and want to do it effectively, you need look no further than the jqPlot jQuery plugin. With the wide range of charts available and the number of options available, you'll be able to locate the perfect elements to display your data.

Hundreds of very practical plugins are available for use in your Web sites and Web applications. However, there is also another group of jQuery plugins that may not be as practical but are fun to use. Let's have a look at some of those next.

PUMPING UP YOUR SITES

For some jQuery plugins, there is a fine line between what is practical and what is cool. Searching the Internet will reveal many jQuery plugins on the bleeding edge of the technology envelope. These kinds of plugins may provide advanced animation techniques that do not work across all browsers or intense data manipulation that prevent the browser from working effectively. Some of these advanced plugins are not viable for everyday use, and many of these progressive plugins are still in the experimental stages, making them unstable.

The plugins you'll use in this section are first-rate and are high-quality enough to be used in your Web sites day in and day out. As with most jQuery plugins, they are easy to incorporate into your designs.

Up first is a way to provide information about the weather at the lodge to visitors of the lodge's Web site.

FIGURE 5.17 The current weather conditions for the lodge.

PREDICTING THE WEATHER

The zWeatherFeed jQuery plugin (www.zazar.net/developers/zweatherfeed) makes it very easy to include weather information from Yahoo on your Web site (**Figure 5.17**). Let's add the zWeatherFeed jQuery plugin to the lodge Web site.

1. Open *chap5/5-7.php* and save it as *chap5/5-10.php*. Include the reference to the zWeatherFeed CSS and jQuery scripts in the head section of *chap5/5-10. php* (highlighted):

```
<link type="text/css" rel="stylesheet" href="css/lamf.css" />

<link type="text/css" rel="stylesheet"
  → href="css/ui/jquery-ui-1.8.12.custom.css" />

<link type="text/css" rel="stylesheet"
  → href="css/tinyTips/tinyTips.css" />

<link type="text/css" rel="stylesheet"
  → href="css/weatherfeed/jquery.zweatherfeed.css" />
```

```
<script type="text/javascript" src="inc/jQuery/jquery
→ -1.5.min.js"></script>

<script type="text/javascript" src="inc/jQuery/jquery-ui
→ -1.8.12.custom.min.js"></script>

<script type="text/javascript"
→ src="inc/jQuery/attractions.js"></script>

<script type="text/javascript"
→ src="inc/jQuery/jquery.tinyTips.js"></script>

<script type="text/javascript"
→ src="inc/jQuery/jquery.zweatherfeed.min.js"></script>
```

2. Include the following jQuery script in the document ready function section of your jQuery code:

```
$('#weather').weatherfeed(
    ['USTX0207'],
    {unit: 'f'}
);
```

The code binds the weatherfeed method to an element with the id of weather, for example, `<div id="weather"></div>`. The options for the weatherfeed method included here are the RSS (Really Simple Syndication) location code and the units of measurement that you want to use, Fahrenheit in this case.

To obtain the RSS location code, go to http://weather.yahoo.com and enter the location information. As shown in **Figure 5.18**, hover your mouse cursor over the RSS icon to see the URL in the status bar of your browser. You will find the location code in that URL, which you can then place into your jQuery weatherfeed function.

NOTE: Be sure to read and understand Yahoo's terms of use policy on weather information.

FIGURE 5.18 Finding the RSS location code.

Because you are providing more information about the lodge to Web-site visitors, most likely you'll want to provide some pictures of the lodge and the surrounding area. A fun way to provide pictures is to use a plugin that will allow visitors to zoom in and view details of the pictures more closely.

ZOOMING IN ON PICTURES

A popular effect on many shopping and photographic Web sites gives users the ability to mouse over and zoom in on an image. Raff Cecco's Cloud Zoom plugin (available at www.professorcloud.com/mainsite/cloud-zoom.htm) is the perfect tool to achieve this effect with jQuery.

1. Open *chap5/5-0.php* and save it as *chap5/5-11.php*.

2. Include the reference to the Cloud Zoom CSS file and jQuery files in the head section of the HTML file (highlighted):

```
<link rel="stylesheet" href="css/primary.css" type="text/css" />
<link rel="stylesheet" href="css/cloudZoom/cloud-zoom.css"
→ type="text/css" />

<script type="text/javascript" src="inc/jQuery/jquery
→ -1.5.min.js"></script>

<script type="text/javascript" src="inc/jQuery/cloud
→ -zoom.1.0.2.min.js"></script>
```

3. Set up a container to hold the photo:

```
<div class="bigPhoto">
```

4. Add the anchor and image tags that reference the large and small photos:

```
<a href='images/lodge_hummingbirds.jpg' class='cloud-zoom'
→ id='zoom1' rel="position: 'inside', smoothMove: 4,
→ adjustX: -1, adjustY:-4">
    <img src="images/lodge_hummingbirds_small.jpg" alt=''
    → title="Hummingbirds at the Lodge" border="0" />
</a>
```

One of the nifty things about this plugin is that you don't have to add any jQuery code to your page. All of the options (highlighted) for the Cloud Zoom plugin are specified in the rel attribute of the anchor tag.

5. Close the container that will hold the photo:

```
</div>
```

6. Center the photo container by adding a CSS rule to *chap5/css/lamf.css*:

```
.bigPhoto {
    position: relative;
    width: 800px;
    margin: auto;
}
```

The zoom effect (**Figure 5.19**) is achieved by having two copies of the image: a small image that is displayed normally and a larger image that will be called by the Cloud Zoom plugin. The larger image (images/lodge_hummingbirds.jpg in this case) is referenced in the anchor tag, and the thumbnail (images/lodge_hummingbirds_small.jpg) is contained within the image tag.

The options specified for this instance of the Cloud Zoom include position: 'inside', which tells the Cloud Zoom plugin to show the zoomed image inside the thumbnail. The option smoothMove: 4 sets up an easing method for the cursor to give the enlarged picture movement a fluid effect. The options adjustX: -1 and adjustY: -4 fine-tune the location of the zoomed image in relation to the thumbnail.

Many other options are available for the jQuery Cloud Zoom plugin that will give you great creative flexibility when you use the plugin in your Web sites.

Another way that you can work with images on your Web sites and applications is to add a background image that resizes with the browser. Let's look at that next.

FIGURE 5.19 The large image is called into the space where the original picture is. Moving the cursor allows users to view various portions of the picture more closely.

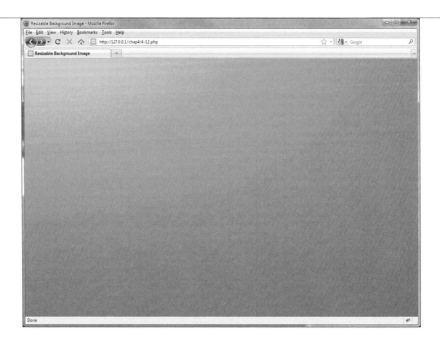

FIGURE 5.20 A gradient-filled background image that is perfectly suited for layering a Web site or application on.

RESIZING A BACKGROUND IMAGE WITH THE BROWSER

For years, Web designers and developers have been looking for ways to improve the backgrounds that their Web sites appear against. Scaling background images is tough to do, especially when you anticipate that the browser window's size might be changed. The jQuery Easy Background Resize plugin solves that problem. In fact, you'll find you'll be looking for ways to use background images in all of your Web sites and applications.

The background resizing plugin combined with one of your images can deliver a subtle (like the gradient background in **Figure 5.20**) or powerful impact to your Web sites and applications. It is by far one of the niftiest plugins you can add to your Web sites.

Developed by J.P. Given, the jQuery Easy Background Resize (available at http://johnpatrickgiven.com/jquery/background-resize) allows you to place a background image on your site and have that background image resize with the browser.

Let's add this plugin to the lodge Web site.

1. Open *chap5/5-10.php* and save it as *chap5/5-13.php*.

FIGURE 5.21 The gradient background has been applied to the body of the Web site. The gradient will expand and contract as needed when the browser is resized.

2. Insert the line that includes the plugin in the head section of the HTML file:

    ```
    <script type="text/javascript" src="inc/jQuery/jquery.ez-bg
     ⟶ -resize.js"></script>
    ```

3. Bind the ezBgResize method to the body tag of the HTML, and designate the path to the image that you want to use as the background:

    ```
    $("body").ezBgResize({
        img : "grfx/lodge_gradient_background.jpg"
    });
    ```

4. Load the page into the browser (**Figure 5.21**) and resize it to see the effect. That's all there is to it!

FIGURE 5.22 A view of the lodge Web site using an image of hummingbirds as the background. This illustrates how easy it is to layer other graphics and Web elements on top of the image.

Once you watch the jQuery Easy Resize plugin in action, you will undoubtedly figure out many creative ways to apply it to your sites and applications. For example, **Figure 5.22** shows that the gradient background has been replaced by the picture of the hummingbirds that was used earlier.

Now that you've made the background spicier, you can add a little plugin to the foreground that will turn some heads.

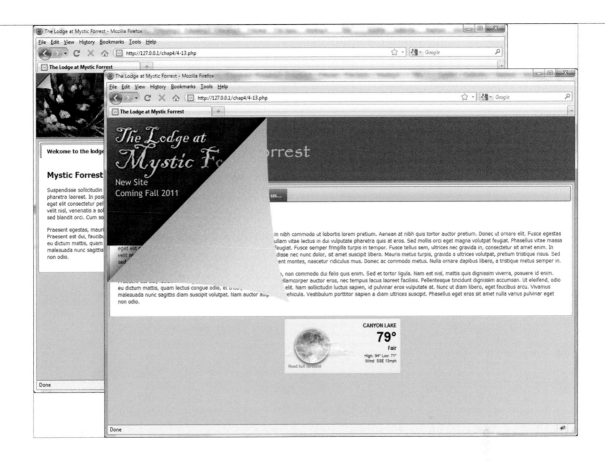

CURLING UP WITH A GOOD WEB SITE

The design of the current lodge site is not as up to date as it could be. The lodge owner wants to let site visitors know that a new Web-site design is coming soon without interfering with the existing site.

In essence, you will be "turning the page" to a new site. A jQuery plugin that supports the concept of turning the page (**Figure 5.23**) is the jQuery Sexy Curls plugin. The information revealed "behind" the curled page is a preview of the new Web site to come.

FIGURE 5.23
The page-curl effect.

Elliot Kember's Sexy Curls jQuery plugin (available at http://elliottkember.com/sexy_curls.html) is the ideal plugin to use to create the page-curling effect. Let's include it in the site now.

1. Create a copy of *chap5/5-13.php* and save it as *chap5/5-14.php*. Make sure that the needed CSS and jQuery files are included in the head section of *chap5/5-14.php*:

```
<link type="text/css" rel="stylesheet" href="css/lamf.css" />

<link type="text/css" rel="stylesheet"
   href="css/ui/jquery-ui-1.8.12.custom.css" />

<link type="text/css" rel="stylesheet"
   href="css/tinyTips/tinyTips.css" />

<link type="text/css" rel="stylesheet"
   href="css/turn/turn.css" />

<link type="text/css" rel="stylesheet"
   href="css/weatherfeed/jquery.zweatherfeed.css" />


<script type="text/javascript" src="inc/jQuery/jquery
   -1.5.min.js"></script>

<script type="text/javascript" src="inc/jQuery/jquery-ui
   -1.8.12.custom.min.js"></script>

<script type="text/javascript"
   src="inc/jQuery/attractions.js"></script>

<script type="text/javascript"
   src="inc/jQuery/jquery.tinyTips.js"></script>

<script type="text/javascript"
   src="inc/jQuery/turn.js"></script>

<script type="text/javascript"
   src="inc/jQuery/jquery.zweatherfeed.min.js"></script>
```

The page curl image is stored in the same folder as the *turn.css* file, *chap5/css/turn*.

2. Add the image tag that holds the "hidden" information prior to the closing body tag:

```
<img id="foldGraphic" src="grfx/lodge_new.jpg">
```

3. Add the jQuery code into the document ready wrapper to bind the fold method to the element that will be shown behind the page curl:

```
$('#foldGraphic').fold();
```

In this case, the element that is bound to the fold method is an image.

The jQuery Sexy Curls plugin is one of the few plugins that I've encountered where developers must open the plugin (located in the folder *chap5/inc/jQuery/turn.js*) to set the options.

4. Open the plugin and locate the section of the code that begins with the comment `//default awesomeness`. (Mr. Kember has a great sense of humor!) The next several lines are the options you can set for the plugin. For this example, the options set are the location of the image used to make the page turn and the starting and maximum measurements:

```
turnImage: 'css/turn/fold.png',
   → // The triangle-shaped fold image
maxHeight: 450,        // The maximum height. Duh.
startingWidth: 40,     // The height and width
startingHeight: 40,    // with which to start
   → (these should probably be camelCase, d'oh.)
```

In addition, the autoCurl function is set to true so that when you mouse over the small curl image, the effect will run:

```
autoCurl: true         // If this is set to true, the fold
   → will curl/uncurl on mouseover/mouseout.
```

5. Load the page into your Web browser and test-drive the curl.

Now that you have installed and configured a number of plugins, you may want to try your hand at developing your own plugins. In the next section, I'll show you how to lay out the basics so that you can make your own jQuery plugins.

ROLLING YOUR OWN PLUGINS

Creating your own plugins can be very rewarding, and it's not difficult to do. Let's write a very basic plugin and put it to use on the lodge Web site.

1. Create a file called **jquery.colorText.js** and save it in the *chap5/inc/jQuery* folder. Start the plugin by declaring a function:

```
(function($){
```

To ensure that you can keep using the familiar dollar sign within your plugin and keep your plugin from colliding with other JavaScript libraries, the plugin framework maps jQuery to the dollar sign. The mapping of jQuery to the self-executing function occurs in the last line of the plugin, (jQuery). This creates a self-executing function called a *closure*.

NOTE: Closures can be complex to understand, but it boils down to keeping local variables for a function alive after the function has been returned. There are volumes of information on closures on the Internet if you're interested in learning more about closures.

2. Add a new function property to the jQuery fn (known as *effin*) object. The name of the property will be the name of your plugin. For the colorText plugin, the user will be able to pass options to the function, so declare that as the argument for the function:

```
$.fn.colorText = function(options) {
```

3. Declare the defaults for each of the options that you will allow the user to declare for the colorText plugin:

```
var defaults = {
    'color'           : '#000000',
    'backgroundColor' : '#FFFFFF'
};
```

The default settings can be extended by passing a JavaScript object literal when the user binds the colorText element to an element. The method that jQuery uses to merge the default options with the passed object literals is the extend method.

The first argument of the extend method is known as the target object. The target object is the object that will be modified when extend is called.

4. Keep the target object blank in this case so that the properties of the defaults and options are preserved. Assign the extend method to the opt variable:

```
var opt = $.extend({}, defaults, options);
```

5. To keep the plugin chainable with other jQuery methods, return the this object while continuing to act on it with methods in your plugin:

```
return this.each(function(){
    $this = $(this);
```

6. Insert the actions that the colorText plugin will perform on the element that is bound to the plugin. In this case, the CSS is being modified (this is not the cleverest plugin in the world) to set the text color and background color of the element bound to the plugin:

```
$this.css({
```

7. Because the default settings and optional settings were merged with the extend method, you can retrieve the values for each property from the object literal stored in opt, like this:

```
        'color': opt.color,
        'backgroundColor': opt.backgroundColor
    });
});
};
```

8. Close out the simple colorText plugin with the proper brackets, and then pass the jQuery object to the plugin:

```
})(jQuery);
```

The plugin is now ready to use.

1. Copy *chap5/5-14.php* and save it as *chap5/5-15.php*.

FIGURE 5.24 The result of applying the `colorText` plugin to elements in the HTML page.

2. Insert the script tag that references the source of `colorText` plugin, just as you've done with all of the other plugins:

```
<script type="text/javascript"
  → src="inc/jQuery/jquery.colorText.js"></script>
```

3. Bind the `colorText` plugin to the h2 element. Insert different values for the color and `backgroundColor` properties to get a feel for how the plugin works:

```
$('h2').colorText({
    'color': '#FFCC33',
    'backgroundColor': '#006600'
});
```

The h2 elements are header elements in each of the tabs of the lodge's Web site. Load *5-15.php* into your browser to see the results shown in **Figure 5.24**.

This `colorText` plugin is a simple example of how to structure a jQuery plugin. You can apply these basic principles to any plugin that you want to create in jQuery. Now that you've incorporated a number of jQuery widgets and plugins into the lodge Web site, you've learned how to start creating your own jQuery to share.

WRAPPING **UP**

This chapter was chockfull of jQuery widgets (from the official jQuery UI library) that you can use to enhance your visitor's interactions with your Web site. These widgets include the Datepicker, Progressbar, and Dialog boxes. All you need to do is include the jQuery UI library file and call each of the widgets, typically with one or two lines of script, in order to make them available in your Web pages and applications.

Next, your eyes were opened to the world-wide widget farm known as jQuery plugins. Developers from across the globe develop and support their own extensions to the jQuery library to provide interactive widgets from tablesorters and tooltips to picture zoomers and graph plotters.

Finally, you learned how to create your own extensions for the jQuery library and gained a template that you can use to support your own library of plugins that you can keep or share with the rest of the world.

In the next chapter, you'll apply all of the skills and tools that you have learned up to this point in the book to create a Web application interface that resembles software instead of a Web site. Let's forge on!

6

CREATING
APPLICATION
INTERFACES

The jQuery library makes creating potent, interactive, Web application interfaces easier by providing methods and functions that excel at supporting the synergy required to turn dull, lifeless, Web application interfaces into full-featured, user-centric powerhouses that can help you to make Web applications interfaces that are intuitive and fun to use.

In this chapter, you'll learn how to apply techniques you have learned in previous chapters along with other jQuery, HTML, and CSS techniques to create a solid foundation for a Web-based application interface. You'll start with the basic markup and style information in detail and add to that as the interface is developed. Along the way you'll learn about advanced techniques for using sprites and AJAX to breathe life into the interface.

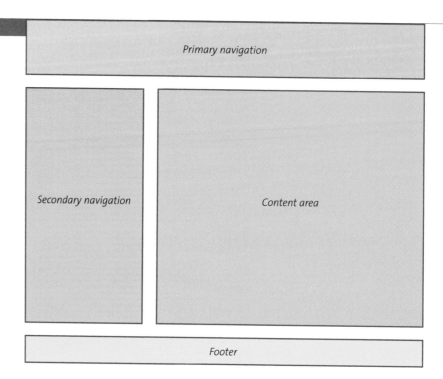

FIGURE 6.1 The basic layout for the Web application interface.

The first step you need to complete for any Web application is to establish the requirements for the application followed by defining a data model. Once those items are complete, you can begin defining the layout for each of the user interfaces required for the application.

When designing the layouts, you must always keep the Web application users in mind. Navigation items must be logically grouped, and content must be consistent. The user should be able to find elements easily while relying on their intuition to guide them. For example, you might have a main navigation component along the top of the interface. When the main item is clicked, secondary navigation is loaded that reflects the choice the user initially makes. The choices must make sense for the user while supporting the actions required by the application.

Once you've decided on the layouts, you can then establish some baseline HTML markup and CSS. The interface that you'll build in this chapter is very basic: Primary navigation will be located at the top of the browser window, secondary navigation will be along the left side of the window, and the primary content will be displayed in a large area on the right (**Figure 6.1**).

The basic layout is completed by providing an area in the browser window for a footer where you can display additional purpose-driven content.

The primary goal for this layout is to keep every element visible on the browser to avoid scrolling. Scrolling will be allowed as necessary, but only within the container that holds more content than can be displayed within that element.

With a layout plan in hand, you'll begin by creating the baseline markup for the project next.

CREATING THE HTML

The HTML markup creates the bedrock on which the rest of the interface will stand. You will define the containers that will hold the content and navigation elements, which will be enhanced by the CSS and jQuery.

After you define the basic HTML markup, you won't have to modify it much except to add declarations for additional jQuery and CSS functions. In keeping with earlier markup layouts, the HTML for the application interface will be very simple. Let's get started.

1. Create a file called *6-1.php* and save it in the *chap6* folder. Open the HTML with the DOCTYPE declaration (in this case the declaration is for HTML5):

   ```
   <!DOCTYPE html>
       <html>
           <head>
               <meta http-equiv="Content-Type" content="text/html;
               → charset=UTF-8" />
   ```

2. Apply the no-cache directives to prevent caching of the application's content. For Web applications, it is desirable that none of the data is cached (held in temporary storage):

   ```
               <meta http-equiv="pragma" content="no-cache" />
               <meta http-equiv="cache-control"
               → content="no-cache" />
   ```

3. Declare the title of the application:

```
<title>jQuery Application Interface</title>
```

4. Create the declarations for the CSS and jQuery/JavaScript files, starting with the style sheet you will create:

```
<link rel="stylesheet" href="css/interface.css"
→ type="text/css" />
<link type="text/css" rel="stylesheet"
→ href="css/ui/jquery-ui-1.8.12.custom.css" />
<script type="text/javascript"
→ src="inc/jQuery/jquery-1.5.min.js"></script>
<script type="text/javascript"
→ src="inc/jQuery/jquery-ui-1.8.12.custom.min.
→ js"></script>
</head>
```

The standard jQuery file as well as the CSS and JavaScript file for the jQuery UI are included in the base markup, so you won't have to worry about adding them later.

5. Add the elements that will hold the navigation and content for the application interface:

```
<body>
    <div id="mainNavBar"></div>
    <div id="content1">
        <div id="contentArea1">
            <!-- nav items -->
        </div>
    </div>
    <div id="content2">
        <div id="contentArea2">
            <!-- content items -->
```

```
            </div>
        </div>
        <div id="footer"></div>
    </body>
</html>
```

The markup contained in the body of the HTML is very simple and easy to read. Each element is clearly declared, and comments make the markup easy to understand.

Next, you'll add some style to the basic HTML markup.

APPLYING THE CSS

The style sheet for your application interface defines the properties for the areas where you'll display content. You need to clearly describe these areas so that the CSS can be effectively applied to your markup.

Let's get the basic CSS properties in place and also include some additional properties that will add borders to each area for visual guidance. After the design is complete, you can remove the borders.

1. Create a file in your text editor called **interface.css**, save it in the *chap6/css* folder, and then establish the overall layout:

```
body, html {
    height:100%;
    margin: 0px auto;
    overflow-y: hidden ! important;
    overflow-x: auto ! important;
}
```

> **NOTE:** The CSS property ! important is always applied to the markup regardless of any other CSS entry that may attempt to override the property. CSS is read from top to bottom, and a CSS property marked as ! important will always be applied no matter where it appears in the CSS document.

```
body  {
    margin: 0px;
    font-family: Tahoma, Arial, Helvetica, sans-serif;
    font-size: 11px;
    background-color: #000000;
}
```

The CSS rules established here ensure that the document body is as tall as the browser window will allow and set all margins to 0. All overflow will be hidden, and no scroll bars will appear on the main body of the interface document. Finally, the background is declared to be black using hexadecimal notation.

2. Set the :focus pseudo selector to have no outline, which will prevent outlines from appearing around clickable items:

```
:focus {
    outline: 0;
}
```

NOTE: A word of caution here; you should never turn off the outline on the :focus element in public Web sites because the element aids in making your Web pages more accessible. If you need your Web applications to be accessible to people using screen readers, you should omit this :focus CSS rule from the CSS document.

3. Set up the container for the secondary navigation. There are two parts, the outer container and the inner container. Declare the outer container first:

```
#content1 {
    width: 20%;
    height: 80%;
    background-color: transparent;
```

```
    vertical-align: bottom;
    float: left;
    margin: 5px 5px 0px 10px;
    position: relative;
    bottom: 0px;
}


#contentArea1 {
    position: relative;
    padding: 10px;
}
```

The outer container #content1 is designed to hold the navigation items that will appear along the left side of the interface. Because the application interface is designed to be fluid (all elements resize with the screen to remain proportional), percentages are used to configure height and width.

4. Construct the CSS to hold the main content with an outer container:

```
#content2 {
    position: relative;
    width: 77%;
    height: 80%;
    background-color: transparent;
    vertical-align: top;
    float: left;
    margin: 5px 5px 0px 0px;
}
```

5. Create the inner container for the main content area, and set the `overflow` property to `auto`. The inner container will have a scroll bar appear when the content is longer than the outer container will allow:

```
#contentArea2 {
    position: relative;
    padding: 10px;
    overflow: auto;
}
```

6. Declare the space for the primary navigation area, including an image that will be used as the background for the navigation:

```
#mainNavBar {
    height: 75px;
    background-image: url('../grfx/large_gray_gradient.png');
    background-repeat: repeat-x;
    padding: 0px 0px 0px 25px;
}
```

7. Create the rule and properties for the footer section:

```
#footer {
    position: absolute;
    bottom: 0px;
    height: 75px;
    width: 99%;
    margin: 5px 5px 0px 5px;
}
```

The footer is aligned to the bottom of the browser window so that the window resizing function, which you'll create later in the chapter, can account for the known fixed space created by the footer element.

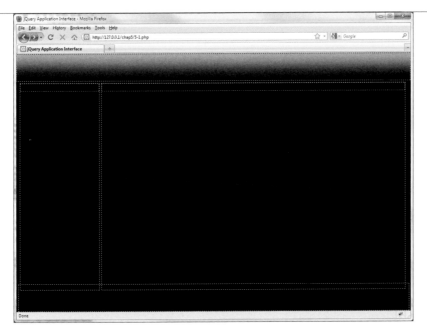

FIGURE 6.2 The primary and secondary navigation areas along with the content and footer areas have been created and are ready for modification.

8. Create the last portion of the CSS style sheet, which contains the rules for the borders that will provide visual guides while the interface is developed:

```
#content1, #content2, #footer {
    border: 1px dashed #FFFF00;
}


#contentArea1, #contentArea2 {
    border: 1px dashed #00FF00;
}
```

After the interface is complete, you can remove these rules.

The base CSS is not complex, yet it is needed to achieve the layout and inter-activity necessary for the application interface.

With the basic CSS and HTML created, you can load *chap6/6-1.php* into a browser (**Figure 6.2**). You should see the yellow borders (outer containers) and green borders (inner containers) for each of the major areas of the application interface.

Notice that some of the navigation and content areas overlap slightly. You'll correct that overlap when you add the jQuery resize function in the next section.

MAKING THE INTERFACE RESIZABLE

For an application interface, it is important that every element be in the proper place at the proper size, not only when the browser is opened, but also when a user decides to resize the browser window. Using jQuery's resize method allows you to accomplish this subtle but important task.

To make sure that the elements are the proper size when the browser window is initially opened, you'll need to know the total height of the window once open. Then you can apply the appropriate heights to the content container elements.

In this exercise, you'll create the jQuery functions to automatically apply the proper heights to all of the container elements based on the size of the browser window when it is opened. Then you'll create the jQuery function that resizes the container elements when the browser window size is changed by the user.

1. Create a new file called ***interface.js*** and save it in the *chap6/inc/jQuery* folder. Then create the document ready wrapper function:

   ```
   $(document).ready(function() {
   ```

2. Use jQuery's height method to get the height of the browser window, and place that information in a variable called windowHeight:

   ```
   var windowHeight = $(window).height();
   ```

3. Set the height of both content outer containers and both content inner containers. The height of the outer containers needs to take into account the height of the mainNavBar (75 pixels) element plus the footer element (75 pixels). Add an additional 25 pixels for padding :

   ```
   $("#content1").height(windowHeight - 175 + "px");
   $("#contentArea1").height(windowHeight - 205 + "px");
   $("#content2").height(windowHeight - 175 + "px");
   $("#contentArea2").height(windowHeight - 205 + "px");
   ```

Make sure that the inner containers, `contentArea1` and `contentArea2`, have their total height set so that they stay inside the outer containers by subtracting an additional 30 pixels from the height of the inner containers.

Next, you'll create a jQuery `resize` function to ensure that the content areas are resized when the browser window size is changed. The same functions that are used to set the content container's size when the browser is opened are used during the resize event, too.

4. Bind the browser window to jQuery's `resize` function:

```
$(window).resize(function() {
```

5. Copy and paste the functions previously used to set the content container heights, and then close the `resize` function with the appropriate brackets:

```
var windowHeight = $(window).height();
$("#content1").height(windowHeight - 175 + "px");
$("#contentArea1").height(windowHeight - 205 + "px");
$("#content2").height(windowHeight - 175 + "px");
$("#contentArea2").height(windowHeight - 205 + "px");
});
```

6. Close out the document ready function:

```
});
```

Now you are ready to include *interface.js* in the HTML declarations.

7. Make a copy of *chap6/6-1.php*, save it as *chap6/6-2.php*, and place a script tag to call the source of *chap6/ inc/jQuery/interface.js* in the head section of the HTML:

```
<script type="text/javascript"
→ src="inc/jQuery/interface.js"></script>
```

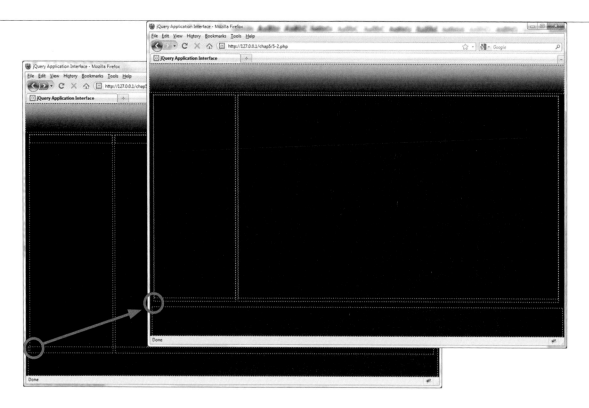

FIGURE 6.3 The content areas overlap the footer element prior to applying the jQuery function that processes the sizes of the content areas.

8. Open *chap6/6-2.php* in a browser window. You'll see that the content areas no longer overlap the footer section of the page (**Figure 6.3**). Resize the browser window to observe the content areas resizing properly.

The basic layout is complete and ready for further development as your Web application interface. Let's start that development by including a robust sprite element as the primary navigation for the application.

NOTE: If you try to make the browser window really small, and for all practical purposes unusable, the content areas will begin to overlap each other again because there is no place for them to go within the space allotted by the browser.

IMPROVING THE
APPLICATION INTERFACE

FIGURE 6.4 The sprite to be used in the Web application interface.

After the basic framework has been established for the Web application interface, you can start to apply the jQuery functions and widgets that will create a rich interactive experience for the application users.

You'll apply some of the techniques that you learned in earlier chapters, including working with events and using the jQuery UI widgets. These techniques and widgets will lend intuitive user interaction to your application while using the efficiency provided by the jQuery library to enable your applications to run smoothly.

To start, let's take the simple sprite navigation technique you learned in Chapter 2 and ramp up the technique's capabilities to make it operate differently, but more effectively, in a Web software application.

CREATING BETTER SPRITES

The interaction of the sprite you worked with previously in Chapter 2 was fairly simple: Hover over an element and it changes. Move the cursor away from the element and it reverts back to its normal appearance. For the Web application interface you are creating in this chapter, the interaction needs to be a bit more complex. Not only will the sprite need to reflect the hover states, but it will also need to reflect a third status (selected) for the area of the application that the user has chosen to work in.

Therefore, you'll need to configure a sprite image with three rows (**Figure 6.4**). You can find this image in the download files in *chap6/grfx/main_nav.png*.

When the mouse cursor hovers over an item in the sprite, the icon will turn yellow and then fade back to gray when the cursor is removed from that icon. This is the same action that occurs with the sprite created previously. The twist is that a selected item does not change when the cursor is hovered over it, and a clicked sprite item will gain the state of selected, turning the icon white.

There are two critical aspects to making the sprite react as you want it to, the CSS and the jQuery. After you have the CSS and jQuery code in place, you'll add the sprite to the HTML. Let's create the CSS first.

STYLING THE SPRITE

Critical to making the sprite work properly is styling the container for the sprite in the page and making sure that each element of the sprite has been defined within the CSS.

1. Create a CSS file called *spritenav.css* in the folder *chap6/css/spritenav*, and set up the first property that will set the height for the sprite. The rule will also have a property to remove default styling from the unordered list that will be used for the sprite:

```
#spriteNav {
    height: 75px;
    list-style: none;
    margin: 0;
    padding: 0;
}
```

2. Make sure that all of the list items float to the left so that they will line up next to each other:

```
#spriteNav li {
    float: left;
}
```

3. Style the anchor tags within the sprite container. The background image for the anchor tags is the graphic that defines the sprite:

```
#spriteNav li a {
    background: url(../../grfx/main_nav.png) no-repeat;
    display: block;
    height: 75px;
    position: relative;
}
```

4. Add the styling for the sprite's span elements. The span elements are the image items in the sprite that appear when the cursor is positioned over the element for hover. The background image for the spans is the same sprite graphic that was used for the anchor elements, *chap6/grfx/main_nav.jpg*:

```
#spriteNav li a span {
    background: url(../../grfx/main_nav.png) no-repeat;
    display: block;
    position: absolute;
    top: 0;
    left: 0;
    height: 75px;
    width: 100%;
}
```

5. Set up the starting base `width` and `background-position` for each item. Each navigation item in the sprite must have a starting width and location. Because the starting position is the top row of the sprite, the *y* coordinate for each item is 0px. All of the sprite items are 100 pixels wide:

```
#spriteNav li a#users {
    width: 100px;
}
#spriteNav li a#notes {
    width: 100px;
    background-position: -100px 0px;
}
#spriteNav li a#stats {
    width: 100px;
    background-position: -200px 0px;
}
#spriteNav li a#processes {
```

```
        width: 100px;
        background-position: -300px 0px;
    }
    #spriteNav li a#security {
        width: 100px;
        background-position: -400px 0px;
    }
```

6. Add the next set of style rules to define the position of the sprite items for the span elements. The span elements provide the hover effect. The sprite items are in the second row of the sprite, so the y coordinate for these has to be -75px:

```
    #spriteNav li a#users span {
        background-position: 0px -75px;
    }
    #spriteNav li a#notes span {
        background-position: -100px -75px;
    }
    #spriteNav li a#stats span {
        background-position: -200px -75px;
    }
    #spriteNav li a#processes span {
        background-position: -300px -75px;
    }
    #spriteNav li a#security span {
        background-position: -400px -75px;
    }
```

7. Prepare the last row of sprite items—the images to be shown when an item is selected—with a *y* coordinate of -150px:

```
#spriteNav li a#users span.selected {
    background-position: 0px -150px;
}
#spriteNav li a#notes span.selected {
    background-position: -100px -150px;
}
#spriteNav li a#stats span.selected {
    background-position: -200px -150px;
}
#spriteNav li a#processes span.selected {
    background-position: -300px -150px;
}
#spriteNav li a#security span.selected {
    background-position: -400px -150px;
    text-decoration: none;
}
```

The styling for the sprite-based navigation is now complete. It's time to turn your attention to the jQuery that will add flair to the sprite.

CREATING THE SPRITE INTERACTION

The jQuery code for the sprite is defined by two functions, one to handle the hover operations and another to handle the clicked or selected sprite item.

1. Create a file named *spreitenav.js* in the folder *chap6/inc/jQuery* and establish the document ready function:

```
$(document).ready(function() {
```

2. Wrap both the hover function and click function into a singular function call to relate them to each other:

```
$(function() {
```

It is not necessary to take this additional step, but it pays great dividends where code organization is concerned.

3. Set up default values for the visibility of the span and span selected elements:

```
$("#spriteNav span").css("opacity", "0");
$("#spriteNav span.selected").css("opacity", "1");
```

4. Begin the hover function by binding the hover method to the #spritenav span element:

```
$("#spriteNav span").hover(function() {
```

5. Create a conditional to test to see if the span element currently hovered over has a CSS class attribute defined for it. If there is no CSS class defined, apply the jQuery animation to fade in the yellow sprite item for this element:

```
if($(this).attr("class").length == 0) {
    $(this).stop().animate({
        opacity: 1
    }, 75);
```

6. Set the element's opacity to 1, fully visible, if there is a CSS class attached to the element that the mouse cursor is over:

```
} else {
    $(this).css("opacity", "1"); // end mousein
};
```

The *mouseover* portion of the hover method is now fully defined, so you'll move on to the *mouseout* section of the hover event.

7. Make the fade-out last a little longer by setting the timing of the fade to 250 milliseconds if the element does not have a CSS class attached to it:

```
        }, function(){
            if($(this).attr("class").length == 0) {
                $(this).stop().animate({
                    opacity: 0
                }, 250);
```

8. Leave the item fully visible regardless of the mouse cursor position if there is a class attached to the element. The class indicates that this item is the currently selected element:

```
            } else {
                $(this).css("opacity", "1"); // end mouseout
            };
```

9. Close out the hover method with the proper closing brackets and braces:

```
        }); // end hover function
```

10. Begin defining the click function by binding jQuery's click method to the #spritenav span element:

```
    $("#spriteNav span").click(function() {
```

11. Remove the selected class from all of the #spritenav elements first, making the current element the only selected element:

```
        $("#spriteNav span").removeClass("selected");
```

12. Use the jQuery addClass method to add the selected class to this element:

```
        $(this).addClass("selected");
```

13. Fade all of the #spritenav elements that do not have the selected class to the state that colors them gray:

```
            $("#spriteNav span:not(.selected)").stop().animate({
                opacity: 0
            }, 0);
```

This will turn the previously selected item back to its gray or nonselected or hovered state.

14. Add the appropriate closing brackets and braces:

```
            });
        });
    });
```

Now that the CSS and jQuery are in place to provide functionality to the sprite, all you have left to do is to add the markup that will place your sprite into the application interface.

ADDING THE SPRITE TO THE INTERFACE

You've done a lot of prep work to get to the point where you can begin adding functionality to the Web application interface. You can rely on the HTML markup and CSS that you constructed earlier to act as a guide for placing new elements into the Web application interface.

1. Make a copy of *chap6/6-2.php* and save it in the *chap6* folder as *6-3.php*.

2. Add the declarations that will link your *spritenav.css* and *spritenav.js* to the head section of your new file's HTML markup as highlighted here:

```
<link rel="stylesheet" href="css/interface.css"
 ⇾ type="text/css" />

<link rel="stylesheet" href="css/spritenav/spritenav.css"
 ⇾ type="text/css" />

<link type="text/css" rel="stylesheet" href="css/ui/jquery-ui
 ⇾ -1.8.12.custom.css" />


<script type="text/javascript"
 ⇾ src="inc/jQuery/jquery-1.5.min.js"></script>
<script type="text/javascript"
 ⇾ src="inc/jQuery/jquery-ui-1.8.12.custom.min.js"></script>
<script type="text/javascript"
 ⇾ src="inc/jQuery/interface.js"></script>
<script type="text/javascript"
 ⇾ src="inc/jQuery/spritenav.js"></script>
```

FIGURE 6.5 Users is the selected item while the mouse cursor is hovered over the Processes item.

3. Locate the `div` element with an `id` of `mainNavBar` and place the unordered list within that element:

```
<div id="mainNavBar">
    <ul id="spriteNav">
```

4. Set a default element to have the `selected` class like this (optional):

```
<li><a id="users"><span class="selected"></span></a></li>
```

5. Make sure that you have a list element for each sprite item:

```
<li><a id="notes"><span></span></a></li>
<li><a id="stats"><span></span></a></li>
<li><a id="processes"><span></span></a></li>
<li><a id="security"><span></span></a></li>
</ul>
</div>
```

The sprite navigation is complete and ready to test.

6. Load *chap6/6-3.php* into your browser to see the navigation (**Figure 6.5**).

The application interface is starting to take shape with the primary navigation in place. You'll no longer need to make changes to the basic layout that you defined in *chap6/6-3.php*. All of the changes to be made from this point on are made in files—the CSS and jQuery files—that will load content into the interface from other files.

Next, you'll learn how to have the primary navigation load the secondary navigation items and primary content.

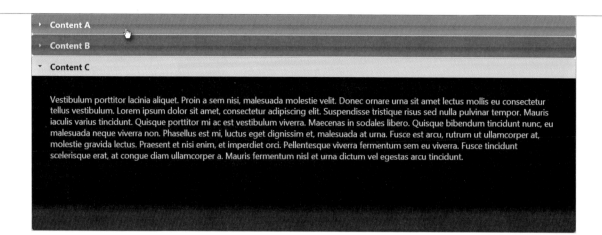

Content A

Content B

Content C

Vestibulum porttitor lacinia aliquet. Proin a sem nisi, malesuada molestie velit. Donec ornare urna sit amet lectus mollis eu consectetur tellus vestibulum. Lorem ipsum dolor sit amet, consectetur adipiscing elit. Suspendisse tristique risus sed nulla pulvinar tempor. Mauris iaculis varius tincidunt. Quisque porttitor mi ac est vestibulum viverra. Maecenas in sodales libero. Quisque bibendum tincidunt nunc, eu malesuada neque viverra non. Phasellus est mi, luctus eget dignissim et, malesuada at urna. Fusce est arcu, rutrum ut ullamcorper at, molestie gravida lectus. Praesent et nisi enim, et imperdiet orci. Pellentesque viverra fermentum sem eu viverra. Fusce tincidunt scelerisque erat, at congue diam ullamcorper a. Mauris fermentum nisl et urna dictum vel egestas arcu tincidunt.

FIGURE 6.6 Clicking on any one of the headers will reveal the content in an accordion by sliding the content and header either up or down as needed.

LOADING CONTENT WITH AJAX

It is easy to target content areas of the Web application interface using jQuery selectors. Once an area is targeted, it is quite simple to use one of jQuery's AJAX methods to call external content into the interface.

You are not limited on the content that you can load into these content areas. Content that you create, as well as jQuery plugins and jQuery UI widgets, are all available to be included into the application interface.

You can also load content into multiple areas at the same time. For instance, with one `click` event you can load content into the secondary navigation area while other content is loaded into the primary content area.

Let's look at a technique for loading a jQuery UI Accordion widget into the navigation area first.

INCLUDING JQUERY UI WIDGETS

A popular widget for displaying a lot of content in a small space is the jQuery UI Accordion widget. The accordion takes up a fixed amount of space, and sliding windows of content are made available by clicking on the headers of the accordion. **Figure 6.6** shows a jQuery UI accordion with three sections and shows the content in section Content C.

You'll use a jQuery UI Accordion widget to facilitate secondary navigation. Let's prepare that widget and then add the call from the primary navigation that will open the accordion.

1. Create a new page called **users.php** in *chap6/inc/nav*. This folder is where all of the secondary navigation files will be stored.

2. Add the following jQuery to bind the jQuery UI accordion method to the element with an `id` of accordion:

```
<script type="text/javascript">
    $(document).ready(function() {
        $('#accordion').accordion();
    });
</script>
```

3. Create the div that will hold the accordion element:

```
<div id="accordion">
```

4. Add a title and the content for each section of the accordion. Note that the title is contained in a header (h3) tag:

```
<h3><a href="#">Manage Users</a></h3>
<div>
    <ul>
        <li><a href="#" id="addUser">Add User</a></li>
        <li><a href="#" id="addUser">Edit User</a></li>
    </ul>
</div>
<h3><a href="#">Manage Roles</a></h3>
<div>
    <ul>
        <li><a href="#" id="addUser">Add Role</a></li>
        <li><a href="#" id="addUser">Edit Role</a></li>
    </ul>
</div>
```

5. Add the last accordion section and close out the accordion element:

```
<h3><a href="#">Manage Groups</a></h3>
<div>
    <ul>
        <li><a href="#" id="addUser">Add Group</a></li>
        <li><a href="#" id="addUser">Edit Group</a></li>
    </ul>
</div>
</div>
```

The jQuery UI library, including the CSS that comes with the library, handles the details of creating the accordion and managing the animation; all that is left to do is to add the jQuery code to load the accordion into the interface.

Rather than creating a new file to create the jQuery code for loading items into the application interface, you'll add the code to the script file created earlier, *chap6/inc/jQuery/interface.js*.

1. Open the *interface.js* file and prepare to add code after the window resize function that was placed in the file earlier.

2. In the first line, bind the click function to the primary navigation element contained in a #spritenav list item anchor tag:

```
$('#spriteNav li a').click(function(){
```

3. Get the value of the id attribute of the item that was clicked and place it in the variable clicked:

```
var clicked = $(this).attr('id');
```

If you're smart about the way you name files, you can use attribute values, like the id attribute in the previous line of code, to aid in creating singular functions that will work over a wide range of events. In this case, the navigation file to be loaded is called *users.php*. That means that the filename relates well to the item clicked.

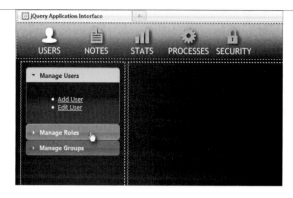

FIGURE 6.7 The jQuery UI Accordion widget is ready to perform as the secondary navigation element for the Web application interface.

4. Create a variable called `loadNav` to hold the filename and path of the file to be loaded. Note that the variable `clicked` is used to complete the text for the path:

```
var loadNav = 'inc/nav/' + clicked + '.php';
```

5. Finish the function by using the jQuery AJAX shorthand method `load` to get the accordion into `contentArea1`:

```
$('#contentArea1').load(loadNav);
});
```

Figure 6.7 reveals the results of your hard work. The jQuery UI Accordion widget is loaded into the secondary navigation area and is ready to use.

It is important to note that you did not have to modify the primary interface because the jQuery UI script file and CSS were already included. Additionally, the technique of binding the UI widget within the file where it is used is the best way to avoid complicated script files.

Additional jQuery will be used in loaded files because it's a better way to organize the application. Keeping the jQuery code isolated within separate files where needed helps to compartmentalize functions for use where they are called instead of having all functions loaded into the interface all the time. Load time is reduced and issues in the code are more easily tracked. The application interface becomes easier to extend as well because new code can be placed into the modules extending the application.

LOADING MULTIPLE ITEMS SIMULTANEOUSLY

With jQuery it is easy to extend functions so that they are capable of processing multiple events at the same time. To demonstrate this capability, you'll create a small form that will be loaded into the primary content area at the same time as the jQuery UI Accordion widget is loaded into the secondary navigation area of the Web application interface.

1. Create a form called *users_search.php* and save it in the *chap6/inc/content* folder.

2. Add the HTML markup for a small form:

```
<form action="#" method="post" id="search_form">
    <fieldset>
        <label>First Name</label><input type="text"
        → name="first_name" id="first_name" /><br />
        <label>Last Name</label><input type="text"
        → name="last_name" id="last_name" /><br />
        <label></label><input type="submit" name="search"
        → id="search" value="Search" /><br />
    </fieldset>
</form>
```

3. Extend the click function defined in the previous section (*chap6/inc/jQuery/ interface.js*) by adding two lines, one line to define the path and filename to be loaded and the other for the load method that applies to the new file:

```
$('#spriteNav li a').click(function(){
    var clicked = $(this).attr('id');
    var loadNav = 'inc/nav/' + clicked + '.php';
    var loadContent = 'inc/content/' + clicked + '_search.php';
    $('#contentArea1').load(loadNav);
    $("#contentArea2").load(loadContent);
});
```

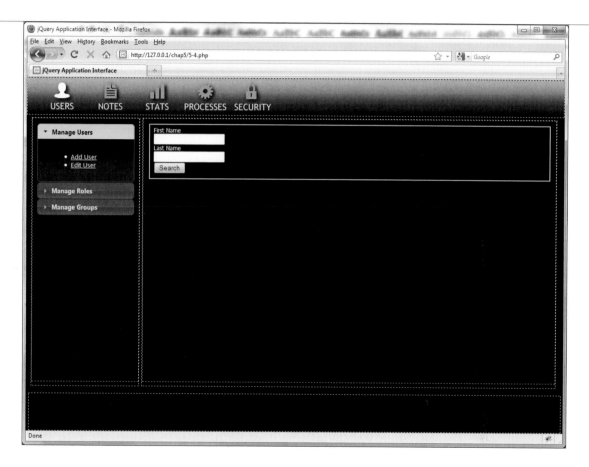

Figure 6.8 shows the result of clicking the *Users* icon in the primary navigation area. The form is loaded into the primary content area, and the jQuery UI Accordion widget appears in the secondary navigation area.

As you can imagine, loading content from various sources into the content areas of a Web application interface is not complex as long as you plan well and keep your code organized. Even large amounts of content are easy to display in the interface.

FIGURE 6.8 Multiple items have been processed by the load method and placed into various portions of the Web application interface.

HANDLING LARGE AMOUNTS OF CONTENT

When you have forms with multiple segments or tabular data that extends for hundreds of rows, it is best to keep that information displayed within the Web application interface without having to scroll the entire content of the window. Scrolling the entire window would move the navigation elements and content identifying headers out of view and possibly confuse users or at the very least cause users to scroll up and down to discern certain information about the data. Any pertinent footer would not be immediately visible, and users might never scroll down far enough to get the information from that element.

That is not to say that you shouldn't build interfaces that cause the entire content window to scroll. If you do allow this in a design element, you need to make sure that there is a way to identify the content and data regardless of where the user has scrolled to. Most designers will do this by including content identification immediately adjacent to the content or by repeating the column headers for tables every few rows.

The CSS that you constructed for the Web application interface provides the proper structure to keep your content available without losing the ability to display the primary and secondary navigation areas as well as the footer should it contain any content.

A large form is available in the download package called *users_add.php* that you can use to test your interface. The form is located in the *chap6/inc/content* folder and contains some jQuery functions, including the jQuery UI Tabs widget.

To load the form into the content area, you'll need to modify the *users.php* file that you created earlier in *chap6/inc/nav*.

1. Open the *users.php* file and add the following (highlighted) jQuery code:

```
$(document).ready(function() {
    $('#accordion').accordion();
    $('#addUser').click(function(event) {
        event.preventDefault();
        $('#contentArea2').load('inc/content/users_add.php');
    });
});
```

The element identified by addUser is bound to the jQuery click method to load the form *inc/content/users_add.php* into contentArea2.

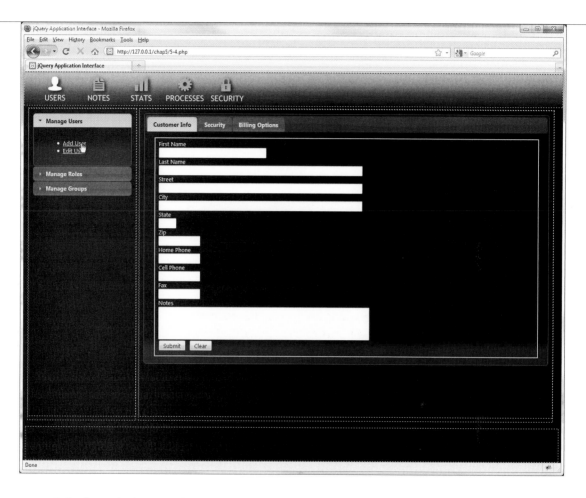

2. Reload *6-4.php* into your browser and click the *Users* icon.

3. When the jQuery UI Accordion widget loads, you can then click *Add User*. The tabbed form should appear in the content area (**Figure 6.9**).

FIGURE 6.9 The form loaded into the Web application interface.

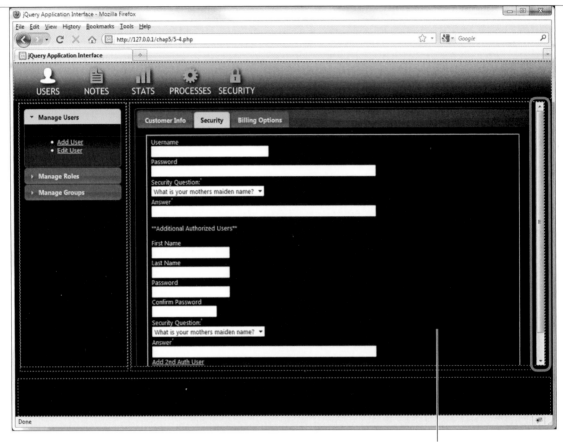

`<div id="contentArea2">`

Content that would normally extend beyond the bottom of the browser window is now contained within the bounds of the content area. That area of the interface will gain a scroll bar when needed. **Figure 6.10** shows the appearance of a scroll bar when the Security tab is clicked due to the amount of content contained on that tab.

Now that you have the basic Web application interface configured and you are able to load content into various areas easily, let's look at some additional features that will enhance the Web application interface.

CONFIGURING ADDITIONAL ENHANCEMENTS

Because you are building a Web application, you'll need to pay attention to how your users are interacting with your application. Are they using the right-click mouse function? Are they clicking the back button instead of using navigation elements? Do you want to limit or modify the user's ability to access the built-in functionality provided by the browser? With the answers to these questions in hand, you can apply some jQuery techniques to accomplish these enhancements.

DISABLING THE RIGHT-CLICK CONTEXT MENU

Many of the action items available from the context menu (**Figure 6.11**) activated by a right-click of the mouse button are not applicable in a Web-based application. Therefore, you can choose to disable the context menu from appearing when the mouse is right-clicked by a user. With jQuery, you only need to apply a short bit of code to accomplish this.

Open the jQuery script file that you created earlier, *interface.js* (located in *chap6/inc/jQuery*), and insert the following code before the closing brackets of the document ready wrapper function:

```
$(document).bind("contextmenu",function(e){
    e.preventDefault();
});
```

The jQuery snippet binds the `contextmenu` event to the document and then applies the `preventDefault` handler to the context menu. This will keep the context menu from popping up when the right mouse button is clicked.

As you might have guessed, some jQuery context menu plugins are also available. These plugins allow you to create custom context menus for your Web applications. Check out my favorite jQuery context menu plugin at http://abeautifulsite. net/blog/2008/09/jquery-context-menu-plugin. Let's add a custom context menu to one of the interface elements.

1. Open *interface.js* in the *chap6/inc/jQuery* folder and place comments around the code that you created to disable the right-click context menu:

```
/*$(document).bind("contextmenu",function(e){
    e.preventDefault();
});*/
```

FIGURE 6.11 The standard context menu in Mozilla's Firefox Web browser. The options would not be very helpful in most Web-based applications.

After you have added the comment, you can save the file. The right-click is now available again; it will be needed for the custom context menu.

2. Open *6-3.php* and save a copy as *6-4.php* in the *chap6* folder. You could add the code to 6-3.php, but for consistency sake (and a backup of your original work) making a copy is the prudent route to take.

3. Add the source calls for the jQuery Context Menu CSS and jQuery files to the head section of *chap6/6-4.php* (highlighted):

```
<link rel="stylesheet" href="css/interface.css"
→ type="text/css" />

<link rel="stylesheet" href="css/spritenav/spritenav.css"
→ type="text/css" />

<link type="text/css" rel="stylesheet"
→ href="css/ui/jquery-ui-1.8.12.custom.css" />

<link type="text/css" rel="stylesheet"
→ href="css/contextmenu/jquery.contextMenu.css" />


<script type="text/javascript" src="inc/jQuery/jquery
→ -1.5.min.js"></script>

<script type="text/javascript" src="inc/jQuery/jquery-ui
→ -1.8.12.custom.min.js"></script>

<script type="text/javascript"
→ src="inc/jQuery/interface.js"></script>

<script type="text/javascript"
→ src="inc/jQuery/spritenav.js"></script>

<script type="text/javascript"
→ src="inc/jQuery/jquery.ContextMenu.js"></script>
```

NOTE: The jQuery Context Menu plugin comes with a folder called images. It is very important that you put this folder into the same folder where you place the jquery.contextMenu.css file.

4. Create a file called **notes.php** and save it in the *chap6/inc/nav* folder.

5. Add the jQuery code to the *notes.php* file for the jQuery UI Accordion widget:

```
<script type="text/javascript">
    $(document).ready(function() {
        $('#accordion').accordion();
```

6. Bind the click method to the addNotes element:

```
        $('#addNotes').click(function(event) {
            event.preventDefault();
```

7. Define the jQuery AJAX load function to retrieve the proper file, and then close the script section of the file:

```
            $('#contentArea2').load('inc/content/notes_add.php');
        });
    });
</script>
```

8. Build the HTML markup for the navigation accordion:

```
<div id="accordion">
    <h3><a href="#">Manage Notes</a></h3>
    <div>
        <ul>
            <li><a href="#" id="addNotes">Add Note</a></li>
            <li>Edit Note</li>
        </ul>
    </div>
</div>
```

Because of the work that you did constructing a solid sprite-based navigation function in *interface.js*, you can now load *chap6/6-4.php* into your browser and click on Notes to make *note.php* appear in the left content area of the interface.

With this working, you can set your sites on creating content that will feature the jQuery Context Menu plugin.

1. Create a file called **notes_add.php** in the *chap6/inc/content* folder.

2. Enter the jQuery code to bind the `contextMenu` to the `noteBody` element:

```
<script type="text/javascript">
    $(document).ready(function() {
        $("#noteBody").contextMenu({
```

3. Assign the id `notesContext` to the menu option of the jQuery Context Menu plugin, and then close out the script tags:

```
            menu: 'notesContext'
        });
    });
</script>
```

4. Create an HTML form for the content of *notes_add.php*:

```
<form action="#" method="post" id="search_form">
    <fieldset>
        <label>Note Title</label><input type="text"
      → name="noteTitle" id="noteTitle" size="64" /><br />
        <label>Content</label><textarea name="noteBody"
      → id="noteBody" cols="64" rows="16"></textarea>
        <label></label><input type="submit" name="saveNote"
      → id="saveNote" value="Save Note" /><br />
    </fieldset>
</form>
```

5. Build an unordered HTML list to contain each of the items to display in your custom context menu:

```html
<ul id="notesContext" class="contextMenu">
    <li class="edit">
        <a href="#edit">Edit</a>
    </li>
    <li class="cut separator">
        <a href="#cut">Cut</a>
    </li>
    <li class="copy">
        <a href="#copy">Copy</a>
    </li>
    <li class="paste">
        <a href="#paste">Paste</a>
    </li>
    <li class="delete">
        <a href="#delete">Delete</a>
    </li>
    <li class="quit separator">
        <a href="#quit">Quit</a>
    </li>
</ul>
```

6. Reload *chap6/6-4.php* into your Web browser and click Notes to load the Manage Notes menu.

7. Click Add Note to see the notes interface appear in the primary content area of the interface.

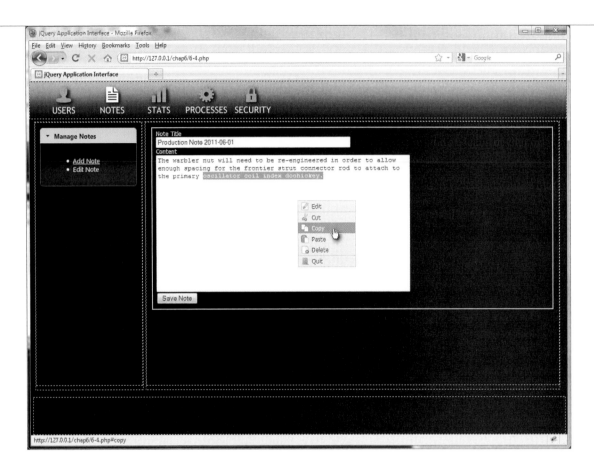

FIGURE 6.12 The new jQuery Custom Context Menu widget is displayed on the Web application interface.

Because you bound the custom context menu to the noteBody element, you can now right-click in the text area of the interface to see the custom context menu (**Figure 6.12**).

Because the jQuery Custom Context Menu is built on a basic unordered HTML list, you can easily bind functionality to all of the elements in the list. The CSS for the jQuery Custom Context Menu is easy to understand and a breeze to extend with additional icons to support any action that you would like to add to the menu. You can declare and assign custom context menus to any of your interfaces.

A more vexing issue than the context menu is the often troublesome back button. Dealing with the back button, and consequently browser history, is an important factor in developing Web application interfaces.

HANDLING THE BACK BUTTON

If you want to be a pro at creating Web applications, you must take into account the browser's back button and the way that the browser manages history. The back button is a Web-browser feature that cannot be disabled, so it is best to incorporate how you will handle the browser's history and how users will operate the back button while planning your Web application.

Rather than dealing with the back button from scratch, a better solution is to turn directly to a jQuery plugin, the Back Button and Query (BBQ) Library by developer "Cowboy" Ben Alman. The plugin is available at http://benalman.com/projects/jquery-bbq-plugin and is a small but very effective plugin that allows you to control the browser history in your Web application. The jQuery BBQ plugin also allows you to set bookmarks for "pages" within your Web application should you choose to allow that feature.

Because of the flexibility of the BBQ plugin, it gives the developer a wide array of options for guiding the user through a Web application's history. The jQuery BBQ plugin will give you the power to manage the history of multiple widgets on a page (e.g., you can control the history of an accordion used for navigation and a tabbed interface used for data entry at the same time). More important, when the BBQ plugin is used correctly, it allows you to leave the back button enabled in your Web application interfaces.

Because there are many ways to apply the jQuery BBQ plugin, I encourage you to visit Ben's Web site, read the documentation, and view the examples. Then download the plugin and build some small-scale examples to get a feel for how the plugin works and the options that BBQ provides. Once you do that, you'll be ready to apply the jQuery BBQ plugin to some of your bigger Web application interface projects.

One last item you need to attend to when developing Web application interfaces is to give users of your application helpful hints.

PROVIDING CONTEXTUAL HELP

When you are designing complex Web application interfaces, you should provide documentation, either printed or online, for your users. The documentation is intended to guide them through the process of using the application. All too often you'll hear people cry, "I don't need to read the instructions!" and users will dive into using the application guided by little more than their intuition.

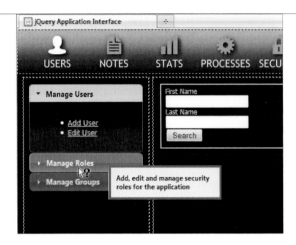

FIGURE 6.13 Hovering above an element on the Web application interface displays a contextual help box.

As the Web application developer, you can give visitors using the application graceful hints when the application may not be quite as intuitive as they (or you) think it is. To do this, you can provide contextual help.

The contextual help function provides users with more information when they hover their mouse cursor over elements that have been assigned a particular class and attribute (**Figure 6.13**). The contextual help window appears only when the mouse cursor lingers over the element to avoid driving users crazy with too much information and too many pop-ups.

To set up the contextual help function, you need to set up the CSS first. Open the CSS file you created earlier, *interface.css*, which is located in the *chap6/css* folder. Add the following two CSS rules at the end of the file:

```
.contextHelp {
    cursor: help;
    position: relative;
}
.contextHelpWrapper {
    width: 175px;
    padding: 10px;
```

```
        border: 4px solid #0066CC;
        background-color: #FFFFCC;
        color: #000000;
        position: absolute;
        top: 20px;
        display: none;
        font-weight: bold;
        font-size: 9pt;
        z-index: 10000;
}
```

The CSS rules change the cursor to alert a user that contextual help is available for an element and style the contextual help box.

Let's create the jQuery function to support the contextual help interface.

1. Open the *interface.js* file you created earlier in the *chap6/inc/jQuery* folder to add the contextual help function.

2. Attach the mouseover and mouseout events to the contextHelp class selector using the delegate method:

   ```
   $('body').delegate('.contextHelp', 'mouseover mouseout',
   →  function(event){
   ```

   The delegate method is used here to ensure that the contextual help function is available for all elements with the proper class, even if those elements do not yet exist in the DOM. For instance, when you load an interface element that has the contextHelp class by clicking a link, the delegate method ensures that the element gets attached to the contextual help function.

3. Test to see if the mouseover event has occurred:

   ```
   if(event.type == 'mouseover'){
   ```

4. Get the `title` information from the element and store it in the variable `this.helpText`:

```
this.helpText = $(this).attr('title');
```

5. Append a div to the current element, which has a class of `contextHelp`:

```
$(this).append('<div class="contextHelpWrapper">' +
→ this.helpText + '</div>');
```

The div is set up to contain the text from the `title` attribute. This text is the contextual help information that will be displayed to the user.

6. Remove the title to thwart the normal behavior:

```
$(this).removeAttr('title');
```

Under normal circumstances, the browser will show a `title` attribute as a small tool tip.

7. Place the `width` of the element that has a class of `contextHelp` into the variable `helpWidth`:

```
var helpWidth = $(this).width();
```

The width information will be used to set up where the contextual help is displayed in relation to the current element.

8. Apply the CSS to define the left edge of the contextual help box based on the variable `helpWidth`:

```
$('.contextHelpWrapper').css({left:helpWidth-25});
```

9. Create a function to hold the `fadeIn` method for the contextual help element:

```
function helpDisplay() {
    $('.contextHelpWrapper').fadeIn(400);
}
```

The `helpDisplay` function will be used by JavaScript's `setTimeout` method to delay the appearance of the contextual help element.

10. Set up the setTimeout method to call the helpDisplay function and delay the visibility by 1250 milliseconds:

```
setTimeout(helpDisplay, 1250);
```

11. Test to see if the mouseout method has been invoked:

```
} else if (event.type == 'mouseout') {
```

12. Restore the title attribute to the contextHelp element so that it can be used again:

```
$(this).attr('title', this.helpText);
```

13. Make the contextual help element disappear by using jQuery's fadeOut method:

```
$('.contextHelpWrapper').fadeOut(100);
```

14. Remove the contextual help box and close out the function with the proper braces and brackets:

```
$('.contextHelpWrapper').remove();
    };
});
```

To use the contextual help function, you apply the contextHelp class along with a title attribute to any element for which you want to display a helpful tip. Look at these two markup examples:

```
<label class="contextHelp" title="Make sure to use a strong
    password">Password</label>

<a href="#" class="contextHelp" title="Add, edit and manage
    application users">
```

FIGURE 6.14 The contextual help function is attached to a form element to prompt the user to provide a strong password.

The class attribute is the hook for the jQuery function, whereas the title attribute contains the text that will be displayed to the user (**Figure 6.14**).

You can adjust the position of contextual help boxes and delay timing to suit your tastes and use in your Web applications and Web sites.

WRAPPING **UP**

The Web application interface has provided you with many additional jQuery techniques to apply to your Web sites and Web-based applications. You can also apply the tools provided earlier in the book to create exciting interactivity for your clients when they are using your applications and Web sites.

In this chapter, you learned how to combine all of your jQuery knowledge into a package that will serve the needs of a highly interactive Web application. You applied jQuery UI widgets and developer plugins, along with hand-crafted jQuery scripts, to create an attractive and useful Web-application template.

Be sure to visit the book's Web site at www.appliedjquery.com for additional examples, articles, plugins, and much, much more about *Applied jQuery*.

> **NOTE:** There are so many more functions and interfaces that you can create for the Web application interface. Use the foundation provided in this chapter to experiment with jQuery events, widgets, and plugins. The interface is far from complete, which will give you many opportunities to apply what you have learned and to learn more about the wonderful world of jQuery.

INDEX

WATCH
READ
CREATE